W

JESUS THE MAN

By the same author:

Legends of the Christchild, The Lutterworth Press, 2003

Stinkie Stevie, Book Guild Publishing, 2006

Collected Poems, Book Guild Publishing, 2007

GOD By Any Other Name Revealed in Myth,
Book Guild Publishing, 2008

JESUS THE MAN

Was There a Historical Jesus?
Who Was the Beloved Disciple?

Christina Sewell

Book Guild Publishing
Sussex, England

First published in Great Britain in 2009 by
The Book Guild Ltd
Pavilion View
19 New Road
Brighton, BN1 1UF

Typesetting in Times by
Keyboard Services, Luton, Bedfordshire

Printed in Great Britain by
CPI Antony Rowe

A catalogue record for this book is available from
The British Library

ISBN 978 1 84624 312 7

To the memory of Jesus of Nazareth,
who, I know, will pardon my intrusion

Acknowledgements

The authors and publishers would like to give special thanks to Tom Harpur, the author of *The Pagan Christ* and Thomas Allen Publishers, Toronto, Canada, for their permission to reproduce copyright material from that book.

Thanks are also due to John Davidson, author of *The Gospel of Jesus*, published by Element Books, HarperCollins Publishers and to J.R. Porter, author of *Jesus Christ – The Jesus of History, The Christ of Faith*, Duncan Baird Publishers and also to Alvin Boyd Kuhn, author of *Who is This King of Glory?*, Academy Press.

If there are any other copyright holders we have failed to mention, or have been unable to trace, the publishers would be pleased to hear from them in order to rectify their omissions in any future edition of this book.

1

Throughout history famous men have been famous for good reason. They have come forward with some arresting new idea, or they have made a major scientific discovery; they have left behind an important historical record, or made an outstanding contribution to the world's golden treasury of works of art; they have been a great military leader or politician; or they have championed the cause of the needy or the oppressed. They have always been famous for what they did, and whatever they did they have stood out in front of their contemporaries on account of it. And naturally their contemporaries, and people in after years, have been interested to learn something of their lives. But it is not their biography that is important; it is their achievement.

Except in the case of one very famous man. With him it is different. Jesus Christ was a great teacher, and his teachings aroused a good deal of interest from the start, but everything he is reputed to have said has been so distorted over the centuries that we cannot now be sure how much of it came out of his own mouth, and although what the Church affirms to be his words are remembered, and valued, and although all the marvels he is purported to have done are willingly accepted by so many credulous people, our chief concern has always been with the man himself; not so much with what he said or what he did, but who he was. Was he human

1

or was he divine? Was he the son of Joseph, the carpenter of Nazareth, or was he the Son of God? Some people have questioned whether he existed at all, or whether everything about him is pure myth, but for all the questions and doubts about him, generated in the first place by the variant accounts of the Gospel writers themselves, and subsequently augmented by all the confusing interpretations and embellishments added by the Church, he is indisputably one of the most famous men that ever lived.

If he ever lived. That is the question. The two authors of *The Laughing Jesus,* Timothy Freke and Peter Gandy, don't think so. According to them the whole story is a myth, as is Jesus himself, and they call upon all believers to 'wake up'. But very many of these 'believers' have woken up long ago, and even dedicated churchmen have had their doubts. The fact is, interesting as their book is, what those two writers say on their subject is nothing new, and they would not deny that. At the very beginning of the twentieth century the German, Arthur Drews, wrote *The Christ Myth* to make the same contention, to prove that Jesus had never existed; and still earlier Ernest Renan (1823–1892) was of the same opinion. And there were others. Many others, and they go much further back. Meister Eckhart (1260–1327), a member of the Dominican Order of Friars Preachers, was branded a heretic for proclaiming that Jesus Christ was not an actual person; he was a mythical figure representing the immortal soul in every man. Eckhart was not the first to say that, or think it. Indeed no rational person, in any age, could accept the story as it stands in the Gospels. It is asking too much of us.

But there are other ways of interpreting the story,

2

and to explore those other ways can be a lifelong adventure. It is not an adventure any explorer sets out on alone. He is always in good company.

And this has always been the case. A Gnostic sect of very early origin called the Docetes did not accept that Jesus ever existed as a man. He could be seen as a real historical figure if that reality were understood in a spiritual sense. Jesus had no physical body, and therefore he could not have suffered for the sake of mankind in the way the writers of the Gospels would have us understand, and since he had not died, literally, he could not have risen again, literally. And all those people living in his own time, and in his own country, who 'heard' him preaching in the temple and 'saw' him perform his miracles, and finally 'saw' him dying on the cross at Golgotha, and afterwards 'saw' him alive again – all those were mistaken; they 'heard' and 'saw' what their ears and eyes told them they were hearing and seeing; they were not to know that everything about the 'man' Jesus was nothing but a grand illusion.

There we have the illusory God-Man. There was also the dual-nature man-God.

In AD 451, when Justinian reigned as Emperor of Rome in his capital of Constantinople, the Fourth General Council of the Church was convened at Chalcedon to endeavour to solve the insoluble problem: was Jesus human or divine? The theologians attending came up with their answer: he was both. He was very God, but on the other side of his dual nature he was also, though above human imperfections, a mortal man. But not everyone agreed. The Monophysites could not accept that Jesus was in any way less than divine, and there have been many people of this persuasion ever since the dawn of Christianity. Just as there have always been those who hold that he was in every way human like the rest of us.

More than a century before the Chalcedonian definition came to be accepted by the Church, the Council of Nicaea, in its effort to combat the Arian heresy, had laid down that the three equal persons of the Trinity constituted the one God, and Jesus Christ, as the second person, was co-equal and divine. Arius had maintained that although Jesus did not share the limitations of the rest of mankind, he was not, as the Son, himself God, but only an aspect of the Father. As such he was a mortal man.

Not surprisingly, confusion led to more confusion. All the different theories put forward over the years have had some plausibility, but the man who has probably done more than any other to uncover the hidden secrets about Jesus Christ is Gerald Massey (1828–1907), a famous Egyptologist who, in his book *Luniolatry*, has this to say:

The insanity lies in mistaking myth for human history or Divine Revelation ... The Gospels do not contain the history of an actual man, but the myth of the God-man, Jesus, *clothed in an historical dress.*

Self-evident to him, no doubt, but others were not so sure.

Massey realised that no one can be sure of anything, but he had carefully weighed all the facts, and of the conclusion he arrived at he was very sure in his own mind. For that sureness he must have owed something to Godfrey Higgins (1772–1833) who, in a less tolerant age than ours, set about a critical examination of the 'evidence upon which our religion was founded'. What he discovered about the whole Bible shocked even him, and what he discovered about Jesus changed his whole

4

understanding of the Christian faith. But he did not go so far as to claim that there was no historical Jesus. Massey went much further and dealt a hefty blow to the established Church. But the Church, for all its bitter backlash, could not prevent him being a great inspiration to many scholars, like Alvin Boyd Kuhn (1880–1963) who carried on in his precursor's footsteps, and who in turn had such a great influence on the present-day writer Tom Harpur, whose book *The Pagan Christ* has made such an impact on me.

The author was an Anglican priest, a former Rhodes Scholar, a professor of Greek and the New Testament at the University of Toronto's School of Theology (TST), and then a religious columnist for *The Toronto Star*. Reading Kuhn and Massey changed his entire outlook on theology. The discoveries he made when he read Kuhn's book gave him such a profound shock that he felt he could no longer carry on in his profession, even though he maintains that the Jesus of his faith is still as real for him as he ever was; he has just come to grasp the reality in a new way. He subsequently became a columnist for the *Toronto Star*. But by his writing he has done more for his faith, as he now understands it, than any clergyman ever could. For the present, this one quotation from *The Pagan Christ* must suffice:

> Very few periods in the history of the ancient world were so well documented as the period when Emperors Caesar Augustus and Tiberius reigned supreme. Yet one amazing fact must be faced: *no contemporary non-Christian writer even knew of Jesus' existence.*

It was to face that fact fairly and squarely that Harpur wrote his book.

Philo Judaeus, the famous Hellenistic Jewish philosopher, makes no mention of Jesus, though he must have heard of him, if he existed, even if the two of them did not live in the same country. Philo lived in Alexandria, but he was a contemporary of Jesus. But then he was a contemporary, or near-contemporary, of many other men of some repute in their own environs, and he may well have considered Jesus not to be worthy of any special note. Although, since Philo's whole endeavour was to demonstrate that the Platonism of the Greeks and the accepted beliefs of the Hebrews were essentially the same as the earlier mystic teaching of the Egyptians, his lack of interest would appear unlikely. But, of course, if Jesus didn't exist, that would explain his silence.

His silence, and that of all the others who might be expected to have made some mention of Jesus, is indeed a matter for concern, but it does not signify that there was never a teacher in Palestine by the name of Jesus, or that those historians and scholars had not heard of him; only that what they knew of him – if they did – did not seem to any one of them to have anything to do with the matter in hand. Indeed, what they could have known of him must have been very far from what we 'know' of him. There was no Church then to tell the story.

Northrop Frye, author of *The Double Vision, Language and Meaning in Religion*, is another writer who joined in the search for the truth about Jesus. According to Johan L. Aitken in his introduction to one of Frye's books, Frye told his students that 'When the Bible is historically accurate it is only accidentally so; reporting was not of the slightest interest to its writers. They had a story to tell which could only be told by myth and metaphor.' So, if Jesus was part of the myth, we should not be looking for any historical figure behind the metaphor. (That is Frye's opinion, not mine.)

Many men, over the years, have said as much. I cannot deal with all of them, but I must mention the one whose argument is the strangest, just because it is so strange. Earl Doherty, author of *The Jesus Puzzle* (a book the importance of which I do not deny), expresses the view that since the name Jesus (Yeshua/Joshua) means in Hebrew 'saviour', the Jesus we know can only be the personification of the universal god who accepts death willingly for our salvation, but never fails to come alive again; the god of all the early Mystery religions. We should not think of Jesus as an actual man.

But Jesus is a very common Jewish name. The index to the works of Flavius Josephus lists fourteen men with that name. Jesus Christ is just one of them. The parents of the others could not have intended to designate their offspring as 'saviour' as Earl Doherty would have it. Although to leave it at that would be doing this writer a very great injustice. His book is extremely interesting, but I am writing about Jesus of Nazareth, not Earl Doherty, so all I will add here is that he does seem to be implying that Jesus is little more than a concept. And indeed that is a fair description of the mythical Jesus. But the man Jesus is something more. The mythical Jesus – the concept – we can revere. The man Jesus we can love.

The other contentions are not so strange, and the contenders have all given of their best; they have all voiced their well-founded opinions. But for more than that, for the nearest thing we have to positive proof, the world had to wait. In the year 1799 a discovery was made which has changed our whole understanding of what Christianity is all about. A French officer of engineers attached to Napoleon's army, M. Boussard, was excavating in the mud of the Nile Delta at Fort St Julien near Rosetta, and there he unearthed a basalt slab which has been appropriately named the Rosetta Stone. But it was not until 1822, twenty-three years later, that the founder of Egyptology, Jean François Champollion, with the help of Thomas Young, succeeded in deciphering the hieroglyphic writing on it. The inscription was in three languages, Egyptian hieroglyphic, demotic and Greek. By a careful correlation of all three texts he finally uncovered what had all along seemed to be an unfathomable mystery. The inscription itself is not of a devotional nature. The sole purpose of the tablet is to honour Ptolemy Epiphanes. But once Champollion had deciphered the hieroglyphs on it, he had the key that unlocked the mystery of other Egyptian texts which were of a devotional nature, such as the Book of the Dead, and what he found there was of the greatest interest to scholars.

But the Church didn't want to know. And that is not so surprising. The Church has always had its own vested interests to protect, and it has never been backward in coming forward. Its grim record of persecution and murder, in the name of a God who is Love and Life, is nothing short of criminal. And it was no kinder to its own adherents, for it did everything in its power to prevent them from ever learning the truth about their faith. Anyone who attempted to reveal that truth was tried for heresy and quickly dispatched. When, more than sixteen hundred years ago, the great library of Alexandria was burnt down because of its alleged inducement to heresy, over 500,000 valuable books and scrolls were lost for ever, which might have been of inestimable value to mankind.

But the Church, unlike its great hero, cannot work

miracles, and slowly but surely the true facts have come to light, even if they are still unknown to the majority of Christians. For the books of men like Massey and Frye and Kuhn are there to be read, and in these more enlightened days there is nothing the Church can do about it. Indeed it may well be that it doesn't want to, for even in that realm there has been great change. Boussard's discovery has been a momentous discovery for us all. I made mine from reading Tom Harpur's *The Pagan Christ*. And in his turn Harpur acknowledges his own huge debt to Gerald Massey and Alvin Boyd Kuhn. According to them Jesus was not the man as we are given to understand. The Christos is the Logos, or Word, dwelling in each one of us creatures, to be reunited ultimately with the Creator. To quote from Harpur's book:

Very early on, in the third and fourth centuries CE, the Christian Church made a fatal and fateful error. Either deliberately, in a competitive bid to win over the greatest numbers of the largely unlettered masses, or through wilful ignorance of the true, inner sense of the profound spiritual wisdom it had inherited from so many ancient sources, the Church took a literalist, popularized, historical approach to sublime truth. What was preserved in the amber of allegory, it misrepresented as plodding fact. The transcendent meaning of glorious myths and symbols was reduced to a farrago of miraculous or irrelevant, or quite unbelievable, 'events'. The great truth that the Christ was to come *in man*, that the Christ principle was potentially in every one of us, was changed to the exclusivist teaching that the Christ had come *as a man*. No other could match him, or even come close. The Dark Ages – and so much more – were the eventual result.

But then the Rosetta Stone was discovered, and the answer to so many questions came with it. And those answers came out of Egypt. I quote from Massey's revealing book *The Natural Genesis*:

> Egypt laboured at the portrait of the Christ for thousands of years before the Greeks added their finishing touches to the type of the ever-youthful solar god. It was Egypt that first made the statue live with her own life and humanized her ideal of the divine. The Christian myths were first related to Horus or Osiris, who was the embodiment of divine goodness, wisdom, truth and purity... This was the greatest hero that ever lived in the mind of man – not in the flesh – to influence with transforming force; the only hero to whom the miracles were natural because he was not human.
>
> The divine child, Horus, descended in his immaterial form to earth from the heaven where he rightly belonged, was born of a virgin and so 'became flesh', a living part of the creation, and in the place of a mortal man he descended into Hades to raise up the dead and bring about their redemption.

And there is more. Much more. For instance, Massey tells us that in the temple of Luxor some extremely interesting carvings have been discovered. There angels appear to shepherds out in the field and reveal to them that a divine child is soon to be born, and an angel announces to a virgin that she is to be the mother of that child. And when the child is born, in a cave, three wise men come and bow down before him. All this was over seventeen hundred years before Jesus was born. And that is just what has been discovered in the

10

temple of Luxor. The myth goes back thousands of years before that.

And it did not stop with Egypt. In Rome, in the catacombs, where the dead in early times were buried deep under the ground, pictures have been discovered of the baby Horus cradled in the arms of his mother Isis, and these and other images of Horus with his solar disc above his head have been mistaken for the infant Jesus with his halo of light. This very natural mistake was made by the early Christians who, in the third and fourth centuries, put the catacombs to such good use, holding their secret meetings there. For them the image could have had no other meaning.

When, upon reading Kuhn's book, Harpur made his discovery, understandably he didn't want to believe it, but faced with the evidence, he had to believe it. It seems clear enough that ancient Egypt was the *fons et origo* of the myth, a myth which spread out in every direction. Its various branches had their little differences, but everywhere the story is in essence the same. A divine saviour comes into the world to suffer and die for man's redemption, but his death is followed by a glorious resurrection.

The ancient Persians worshipped Mithras, their solar god, and in their scriptures, the Zend-Avesta, Zoroaster (Zarathustra), the sixth century BC founder of their religion, Zoroastrianism, speaks of a divine child, a saviour, born of a virgin. Zoroaster's priests, the Magi, or wise men, were Gaspar, 'the White one', Melchior, 'the King of Light', and Balthazar, 'the Lord of Treasures'. All these are common appellations for Mithras. And Zoroaster is recorded as addressing the three of them:

'A star shall go before you to conduct you to the place of his nativity, and when you shall find him,

11

present to him your oblation and sacrifices, for he is indeed your lord and an everlasting king.'

Much later than Zoroaster, another Persian, Mani, a mystic of the third century AD, while insisting that his message was no different from that of Jesus, averred that Jesus' teachings had suffered so much at the hands of the evangelists that their real meaning lay hidden under a dark cloud. He made it his mission to uncover that meaning – the meaning of the words spoken by a man he certainly believed had actually existed.

In the famous Indian religious poem, the *Bhagavad-Gita*, Song of the Blessed, Krishna, an avatar of the Hindu god Vishnu, appearing as a mortal man and a charioteer, announces to the warrior chief Arjuna:

'I am the letter A',

and:

'Of all creations I am the beginning and the end.'

Just as Jesus says:

'I am the Alpha and Omega'.

And in Ceylon a divine child named Salivahana was born of a virgin, and he too was the son of a carpenter!

I could go on and on. Harpur lists other similarities between the great archetype, the Egyptian Horus, and Jesus. The comments made, as well as the list, are his:

- Like the 'star in the east' of the Gospels, Sirius, the morning star in Egypt, heralded the birth of Horus.

12

- Horus was baptized in the River Eridanus (Jordan) by a god figure named Anup the Baptizer (John the Baptist), who was later decapitated.
- Like Jesus, Horus had no history between the ages of twelve and thirty.
- Horus walked on water, cast out demons, and healed the sick.
- Horus was transfigured on a mountain; Jesus took Peter, James and John into 'a high mountain' and was transfigured before them.
- Horus delivered a 'Sermon on the Mount' and his followers faithfully recounted the 'Sayings of Iusa' (or Jesus).
- Horus was crucified between two thieves, buried in a tomb, and resurrected. His personal epithet was Iusa (or Iusu), the 'ever-becoming son' of Ptah, or the Father.
- Horus was the good shepherd, the lamb of God, the bread of life, the son of man, the Word, and the fisher; so was Jesus.
- Horus was not just the path to heaven but the way by which the dead travel out of the sepulchre. He was the god whose name was written as the 'road to salvation'; he was thus 'the Way, the Truth and the Life'. *Therefore, the key verse of conservative orthodoxy today was sourced in Pagan roots.*
- The Creed says that Jesus descended into hell, or (better) Hades, but so too did Horus before him. Both went to preach to the souls in prison. Both were 'dead and buried', but only figuratively. Again, this is simply a metaphorical description of the descent of the divine into matter – into human beings, in fact. As Kuhn sharply observes, 'It has absolutely nothing whatever to do with

13

a literal hillside grave.' The death of the god is his self-giving to mortals. That's why every ancient religion had at its heart a dying or dismembered/disfigured deity. One of humanity's first mythical saviour figures, Prometheus, was pinned by the wrists and ankles to a rock in the Caucasus Mountains where his liver was torn out by a vulture.

- Jesus came in the name of the Lord. He was called Kyrios, or Lord. Horus too was 'the Lord' by name.
- Like Jesus, Horus was supposed to reign for one thousand years (i.e., to usher in a millennium).
- Horus came to seek and to save what was lost. We are reminded of the Gospel parables of the lost sheep, the lost coin, and the 'lost' son.
- In the Gospels, it is the women who announce the Resurrection. 'The goddesses and the women proclaim me when they see me,' shouts Horus as he rises from the tomb 'on the horizon of the resurrection'.

And this list is by no means complete. If it were it would be as long as the Gospel story. But the single point that stands out is this: Horus, the ancient Egyptians' Supreme Being, had other names, one of which was Iu-em-hetep or Iusu, a fact we learn from the famous historian Heroditus. Horus was the Egyptian Christos.

Faced with these facts, is it any wonder that the Church had its heretics? For hundreds of years scholars have made their protest. But the Church has also had its defenders. Justin Martyr, a famous early Church Father, declared that the wicked devils had cooked up the whole story in ancient times in order to get in first and so discredit Jesus when he should come into the

14

world. And when the Pagans accused Christianity of gross plagiarism, he was ready with his answer. Everything the Christians taught about Jesus, the Son of God, born of a virgin, even what the Bible had to say about his crucifixion and resurrection, was in substance the same as what their religion taught about their gods. Only the Christians had the right God.

Well, that was no sort of answer. Justin was in a fix and there was no way he could wriggle out of it. He was saying just what the Pagans were saying. The thievery couldn't be more obvious.

And Quintus Tertullian, a famous Carthaginian theologian, said much the same as Justin, that the devil by 'the mysteries of his idols' was bent on imitating the Christian Mysteries.

> He baptizes his worshippers in water and makes them believe that purifies them from their crimes! Mithras sets his mark on the forehead of his soldiers; he celebrates the offering of bread; he offers an image of the resurrection ... he limits his chief priests to a single marriage; he even has his virgins and ascetics.

The opposing party has continued to maintain that Christianity has all along been guilty of plagiarism, and Tom Harpur says that in his view this is obviously the truth. In his book *The Pagan Christ* he says this:

> Everything – from the star in the east to Jesus' walking on water, from the angel's pronouncement to the slaughter of the innocents by Herod, from the temptation in the wilderness to the changing of water into wine – already existed in the Egyptian sources. Egypt and its peoples had knelt at the shrine of the Madonna and Child, Isis and Horus, for many

long centuries before any allegedly historical Mary lifted a supposedly historical Jesus in her arms. But for all those centuries before the translation of the Rosetta Stone by Champollion in 1822, the ancient key to all this Egyptian material had been lost. Centuries of blissful ignorance went by. Now, since the translation of the books of old Egypt – the Egyptian Book of the Dead, the Pyramid Texts, the Amduat, and the 'Book of Thoth', for example – there is irrefutable proof that not one single doctrine, rite, tenet, or usage in Christianity was in reality a fresh contribution to the world of religion.

And:

The cross ... was a feature of ancient religion for a vast span of time prior to the Christian era.

And:

The Greek monogram comprising the first two letters of the word for Christ (*chi* and *rho*), letters often superimposed on each other in church ornamentation – was also pre-existent to Christianity. It appears on the coins of the Ptolemies and even those of King Herod the Great almost forty years BCE. Herod was made king of the Jews by the Romans in 40 BCE, and he reigned until 4 BCE. The Emperor Constantine the Great put this monogram on the labarum, or standard, of his legions after his famous victory at the Milvian Bridge three hundred years later. Thus he linked the Church to his political and military power, and all who rebelled against the new Catholic or universal orthodoxy were labelled heretics.

16

When Gerald Massey looked at the stories of the Egyptian sun gods, Osiris, Horus, and Ra, who in fact are all the same god, he had drawn the inevitable conclusion: Egypt was both the father and the mother of the myth: the myth of the Godman who died for us and rose again in glory, whether he is the Egyptian Horus, or the Greek Dionysus, or whether he is the Persian Mithras, or any other god of the various Mystery religions. Or Jesus.

The Egyptian Christ was Horus, the solar god, though at different times he was Ra or Osiris. All were names for the one Great God. The meaning of the message on the Rosetta Stone, and the carvings and zodiacs in the temple of Luxor, were more than a discovery; they were a revelation. And Massey's was a very great achievement in pointing out the many similarities between the myths of the Egyptians and the Christians. And he said this:

> We can now state that the Gospel 'life' of Jesus had already been written, in substance, at least five thousand years before he came.

And as we have already noted, Kuhn added still further evidence to back him up. Both men have clearly demonstrated that astrology has from the first been behind all religion.

In *Who is this King of Glory?* Kuhn says:

> All that went into the making of the Christian historical set-up was long pre-extant as something quite other than history; was in fact expressly non-historical in the Egyptian mythology and eschatology. For when the sun at the Easter equinox entered the sign of the fishes (Pisces) about 255 BCE, the Jesus

17

who stands as the founder of Christianity was at least 10,000 years of age and had been travelling hither as the Ever Coming One through all preceding time... During those 10,000 years, that same incarnation of Iusa (or Horus), the Coming Son, had saturated the mind of Egypt with its exalting influence. Little did men of that epoch dream that their ideal figure of man's divinity would in time be rendered historical as a man of flesh.

Though I have to say here that I very much doubt if the average less intelligent Egyptian would have been any different from the same class of person in our time.

And long before Kuhn, St Augustine (354–420 CE), Bishop of Hippo and famous Doctor of the Church, actually said this in his *Retractiones*:

The very thing which is now called the Christian religion existed among the ancients also, nor was it wanting from the inception of the human race until the coming of Christ in the flesh, at which point the true religion which was already in existence began to be called Christian.

St Augustine was not quite right about this. The 'true religion' was not called Christian until after Jesus' death. The Acts of the Apostles inform us that in Antioch the disciples were for the first time called Christians. But, coming from a bishop, that assertion of Augustine's must have come as a shock to his readers. As it did to Harpur. The reality is – the reality behind all the conjecture and debate – what is true is true for ever, but at times old truths need to be revived, and told in a new way, and the old truths taught by Jesus did seem to his hearers to be something new.

I quote again from Harpur:

> When we review the exact parallels between early saviour stories and the sayings and actions of Jesus, it's more than obvious that what we're dealing with is another variant of the overarching archetypal theme of the same mythos in all ancient religion – only this time in Jewish dress.

And:

> The body of material regularly used in the ceremonial dramas of the widespread early Mystery Religions around 1200 years BCE makes up in general the series of events narrated in the New Testament as if they were Jesus' personal life story.

A story which, Harpur says, is 'a profoundly spiritual allegory of the soul'.

And Kuhn:

> A story and a whole range of symbols meant to relate to our own inner selves have been taken as purely historical facts about a distant, inhuman person who was God-in-disguise.

And finally, to return to Harpur:

> Jesus lives on for us, but in a new way.

That new way of seeing things is what concerns us now. Many men have joined in the quest. They have all striven to uncover the truth behind the Scriptures and to encourage their readers to think for themselves.

There was Godfrey Higgins (1771-1834) whose far-searching work on the origins of religions so impressed Kuhn, and, later, Albert Schweizer (1875–1965), who made the bold claim that there was no historical Jesus; and Sigmund Freud (1856–1939), who accused the Bible of being a 'total plagiarism' of the mythologies of Egypt and Sumeria. And since their time others have followed in their track. The heretics have not given up. And many of them are of the same opinion, that Jesus never existed. He is, they say, just a myth, the creation of St Paul who claimed to have seen him in a vision just when he was on his way to Damascus to hunt down Jesus' followers.

But from what we are given to understand about Paul, that is far from the truth. Paul was a Gnostic, and what he taught was rather different from the teaching of Jesus – or at least from his teaching as revealed in the Gospels. In his letter to the Galatians Paul says:

> I would have you know, brethren, that the Gospel which was preached by me is not man's gospel. For I did not receive it from man, nor was I taught it, but it came through a revelation of Jesus Christ.

> Galatians 1: 11–12

What he saw in his vision could hardly have been Jesus 'in the flesh', seeing that he had never set eyes on Jesus. What he 'saw' was the Logos, the 'Christ within', which is without substance, yet is more real than so-called reality. He was more interested in Gnosticism than in Jesus' teachings, and more interested in Paul than in Jesus of Nazareth. And the fact that he never had much to say about Jesus has persuaded some scholars that Jesus could never have existed. For surely the man who had seen him in a vision, and was setting out to make Christians of the Gentiles, would have had a good deal to say about his Master's acts and sayings. But then, if he didn't know that Jesus had actually existed, why would he have called him 'the Lord Jesus Christ'? And why had he formerly been so hell-bent on persecuting his followers? And how is it that he did more than anyone else to establish a faith based on a firm belief in the physical identity of a man of whom he knew nothing and didn't even believe had existed? Paul's Gnostic beliefs, on their own, however appealing to the intelligentsia, would never have attracted such large numbers of ordinary people.

No doubt he did not believe in the physical reincarnation of Jesus, as did so many of the early Christians who expected to see him again at the world's end which was to come at any time; but that does not mean that he didn't believe in his existence, and in the fundamental truth of his message. He may not have been particularly interested in the man himself; rather in the spiritual being behind the flesh. And the people he addressed would not have needed to be given the details of Jesus' life. For them, as for him, the fact of Jesus' actual existence was never in dispute.

It was Jesus' message that chiefly concerned Paul. Although it would appear that he held his own mystical wisdom in higher esteem than the down-to-earth wisdom of Jesus. Jesus spoke in parables so that anyone would understand his meaning. Paul spoke as a scholar to scholars, disregarding all those who could not understand him. He wanted to show Jesus as he saw him, the mystical figure he undoubtedly was, but he was also the plain man who may have held less interest for Paul, but whose existence, together with that of his mother, he never denied. And those two have come to mean more to more people than any other mortals before or after.

Paul has not so many adherents today as formerly, and many who have listened to Jesus have given up on Paul, as, indeed, many have given up, or partly given up, on Jesus. Heresy is no longer condemned. Heretical books are avidly read, and often end up as best-sellers. Some of them, like John Davidson's *The Gospel of Jesus – In Search of His Original Teachings*, can be very persuasive. But they don't convince me.

I *cannot* believe that Jesus never existed, or that he was not a real man. For me he is realler than real, if I may use that form of the comparative. In truth there can be no comparison. Things are either real or unreal. But if I am to say what I really mean, I see no other way round it. You and I are real, as the world sees it; fairies are unreal. But fairies exist and will always exist in the minds of children, whereas, in a very short time, you and I will be no more than a memory. The 'real' person and the fairy of story-books are each in a different category. But Jesus is not in any category. He is in a class of his own. And whatever the truth about him might be, or might not be, what I see in my mind's eye is standing before me now, as real as any one or any thing I see with my seeing eyes, and I cannot believe that he isn't *there*.

He was there for Paul. Paul was interested in the mythical Jesus rather than the historical one. He didn't really do Jesus justice, and I must say that any man, however well-meaning, who sets out to persecute those he doesn't agree with, or who, however intelligent, is a visionary, is not a man I could put my whole trust in. But Paul knew that the historical Jesus had existed, and nothing he ever said is indicative of anything to the contrary.

And so, I repeat, I do believe that Jesus existed. He was a real man who lived in Palestine in the reign of the Emperor Tiberius. No rational person can be expected to believe all that has been written about him. Of course much of it is pure myth. But he himself is no myth, though certainly he is the subject of a grand myth, which in a literal sense must be accounted nonsense. He was very real; the myth was built up around him.

The best argument I have yet found to prove me wrong must be quoted here. It is from Gerald Massey's *The Historical Jesus and the Mythical Christ*:

> The general assumption concerning the Gospels is that the historical element was the kernel of the whole, and that the fables accreted around it; whereas the myths, being pre-extant, prove that the core of the material was mythical, and it then follows that the 'history' is incremental... The worst foes of the truth have ever been the rationalizers of the mythos.

Yes, the core of the material is mythical, and I do not believe that Jesus of Nazareth *actually* played any part in the myth. The myth was *there* long before he was born. But that doesn't mean that an ordinary man called Jesus of Nazareth never existed. If later men have built on his actual story to relate it to the myth, they have not been entirely successful. The real man stands out above it all. And if Jesus is reported to have said at times things which imply that he was, or was claiming to be, the mythical hero, there is no proof that he ever said those things. The myth-builders put the words into his mouth.

And the myth has worked wonders for him. If he could come back and read the half of what has been written about him, he would never recognize himself in the man portrayed. Admittedly Jesus was no ordinary man; he was just the sort the builders of a myth might choose for their subject, and for all the reasons why they shouldn't, which I shall be pointing out to you, he was the aspiring star who got the part. They could not fail to see his vast potential. But I do believe he was a real man and worthy of the build-up.

His story does contain some historical details which are hardly appropriate components of a myth, though they do constitute the setting for the account of the life of the real man behind the myth.

The census had to be brought in if Jesus was to be born in Bethlehem, the city of David. Augustus Caesar, who was Emperor before Tiberius, sent out a decree that all the world should be taxed, and as his subjects must report to their birth city for enrolment, Joseph, who lived in Galilee, had to go with his heavily pregnant wife Mary to Bethlehem, and there Mary's baby was born. And so, because his father's birth city was Bethlehem, and he was therefore a descendant of King David, Jesus could claim to be a descendant of King David too. It was a clever ruse, but on two points it falls way short of the target. Many other people had been born in Bethlehem, but they could not all have been descendants of a king. And anyway, Joseph was not supposed to be Jesus' real father. (Although those who made this objection were early on refuted with the contention that Mary was descended from King David.)

Then there are some rather strange remarks attributed to Jesus during his ministry:

While he was still speaking to the people behold, his mother and his brothers stood outside, asking to speak to him. But he replied to the man who told him, 'Who is my mother, and who are my brothers!' And stretching out his hand toward his disciples, he said 'Here are my mother and my brothers.' For whoever does the will of my Father in heaven is my brother, and sister and mother.'

Matthew 12: 46–50

And:

'He who loves father or mother more than me is not worthy of me; and he who loves son or daughter more than me is not worthy of me.'

Matthew 10: 37

All very well in one sense, but callous and quite uncalled-for in another. No reasonable person would expect so much of any parent.

Of course it is highly unlikely that these were Jesus' actual words. People often write (and even alter what others have written) to suit their own ends. I doubt if the history books in use by German schoolchildren are the same as those in use by English children today. There Hitler is the problem. The Church too has had its problems, and we cannot be sure that anything in the Bible can be taken at face value. To quote the authors of *The Laughing Jesus*:

The process that created the New Testament was uncannily like that which produced the Old Testament. Both were put together by sectarian Literalists intent on creating and maintaining their own power and authority. Both contain the remains

25

of Gnostic myths which have been buried beneath accretions of blatant political propaganda. Both are riddled with contradictions and anomalies because they have been altered and amended by so many editorial hands. The Literalists' Bible is not holy scripture. It's an unholy mess.

And so it is, but if you poke about in that mess you may discover a rich treasure. And you may find a way to separate the truth from the lies. For instance, if, after duly considering what Jesus had to say about loving your family members as told in the Gospel of Matthew, you go on to read the Apocryphal Gospel of Thomas, you will find there a much more humane Jesus:

'He who does not dislike his father and his mother in my way will not be able to become my disciple; and he who does not love his Father and his Mother in my way will not be able to become my disciple; for my mother has begotten me, but my true Mother gave me Life.'

Thomas puts it more sympathetically, and, I think, more plausibly. He shows a greater understanding of Jesus than the canonical Gospel writer. For although Jesus called God his Father, and himself his Son, the ordinary father-and-son relationship was not what he had in mind, and even the most ignorant among his audience would have realized that. Jesus must have had a real father (for all the talk to the contrary) and he knew that Mary was his mother. But just because she gave him life, he didn't *have* to give her all his love. And the same goes for Joseph.

So Thomas has vindicated Jesus in that instance. But there are other instances where the words spoken by

Jesus are not what we would expect. How about this from Luke:

> To another he said, 'Follow me.' But the man said, 'Lord, let me first go and bury my father.' But Jesus said to him, 'Leave the dead to bury their dead; but as for you, go and proclaim the kingdom of God.' Another said, 'I will follow you, Lord, but let me first say farewell to those at my home.' Jesus said to him, 'No one who puts his hand to the plough and looks back is fit for the kingdom of God.'

Luke 9: 59–62

And this from Matthew:

> In the morning as he was returning into the city, he was hungry. And seeing a fig tree by the wayside, he went to it and, finding nothing on it but leaves, he said to it, 'May you bear no fruit ever again.' And immediately the fig tree withered away.

Matthew 21: 18–19

If this story does not fit well into the historical account, neither does it say anything for the loving kindness of the mythical god. As in the other instances quoted, Jesus is portrayed as a mortal man with all his faults and foibles.

Though even the imperfect human side of Jesus can be misunderstood. In her extremely interesting book, *Jesus The Man*, Barbara Thiering, having made a thorough search through the Dead Sea Scrolls, with all the light they throw on the ideas and practices of the Jewish sect of the Essenes at Qumran, now gives this story its proper interpretation. The Figtree was the name given to a breakaway group from the ascetic sect of the Therapeutae, a group consisting of three opponents of John the Baptist, namely Herod Antipas, Ephraim and Manasseh, and when Jesus withered the fig tree with his curse because it bore no fruit, he was actually condemning those three men of whose principles he strongly disapproved. There can be little doubt that this must be the true meaning of the story, but I have chosen to see Jesus as the Gospels reveal him. Some of their content makes sense and some doesn't, but even in non-sense there is often a kind of truth. If Jesus was a member of the Essene community, brought up by his Essene father, Joseph, to regard himself as the one destined to inherit the primacy of his royal ancestor, King David, then we should indeed have to see him in a new light; but just because we cannot believe every word of the Gospel story, it does not follow that we should put our complete trust in any scroll. There have never been so many different renderings of any story as there are of the story of Jesus, and many of them are very convincing, but they can't all be the whole truth. Most probably none of them can claim to be that. I shall stick with my personal choice.

The story of Lazarus presents us with another inconsistency:

When Jesus saw her [Mary, Martha's sister] weeping, and the Jews who were with her also weeping, he was deeply moved in spirit and troubled; and he said, 'Where have you laid him?' They said to him, 'Lord, come and see.' Jesus wept.

John 11: 33–35

Now if Jesus could raise Lazarus from the dead, and presumably knew that he could, why should he weep?

Jesus is said to have brought more than one person back from the dead. And this fits well enough into the myth. But if there had been any decisive evidence that he actually possessed this miraculous power, if only as part of the myth, then surely the Pharisees and Sadducees (also as part of the myth) would have acclaimed him as the Messiah. But in the absence of evidence they did no such thing, and they didn't like the speed with which such doubtful stories were going about among the common people. The stories were made up, but Jesus was real, and their hostility was real.

In Matthew's Gospel we find yet another inconsistency in the 'myth' notion. At the time of Jesus there was a general expectation of an imminent end of the world; although, it is true, the original Greek text of the Scriptures seems to be speaking of the end of the age, or cycle, not the end of the world. (The ending of the age of Pisces and the beginning of the age of Aquarius.) Even so, many people were apprehensive, and Jesus kept on about it, urging all sinners (that is, all people) to repent before it was too late. And naturally his disciples would have been in high hopes that their Master would be able to tell them when exactly the end would come. But when Jesus was questioned by them on the subject, he soon realized that there was nothing for it but to confess his ignorance. This was his answer:

'Truly I tell you, this generation will not pass away till all these things take place. Heaven and earth will pass away, but my words will not pass away.

But of that day and hour no man knows, no,

29

not even the angels of heaven, nor the Son, but the Father only.'

This must have disappointed his disciples, and surprised them not a little. Would a God-man have to confess his ignorance of anything at all? At times Jesus did get carried away on a whimsical flight of fancy, but for all that he must have known perfectly well that he was no more than a man. Also, if he believed, along with the rest, that the end of the world was at hand, he could not have been more mistaken. The God-man did not exist, but the fallible Jesus did.

Outside the Gospels there is further evidence that he existed. The famous Jewish historian Flavius Josephus, who lived just after the time of Jesus and would probably have heard a good deal about him, and would, one would suppose, have thought much of it worthy of comment, has very little in fact to say about him. But he does say this:

Now, there was about this time (in the reign of the Emperor Tiberius) Jesus, a wise man, if it be lawful to call him a man, for he was a doer of wonderful works – a teacher of such men as receive the truth with pleasure. He drew over to him both many of the Jews, and many of the Gentiles. He was the Christ; and when Pilate, at the suggestion of the principal men amongst us, had condemned him to the cross, those that loved him at the first did not forsake him, for he appeared to them alive again the third day, as the divine prophets had foretold these and ten thousand other wonderful things concerning him; and the tribe of Christians, so named from him, are not extinct at this day.

Not much, but, I would say, not unimpressive, especially coming from a Jew.

If it did. There are some who have suggested that the original text may have been tampered with in the interests of the Church. And indeed it may well be, as has been suggested, that his words should read more like this:

Now there was about this time Jesus, a wise man, and a doer (or so it was claimed) of wonderful works – a teacher of such men who are given to delusion. He drew over to him both many of the Jews, and many of the Gentiles. He said he was the Christ, and when Pilate, at the suggestion of the principal men amongst us, had condemned him to the cross, those that loved him at the first did not forsake him, for he appeared to them alive again the third day (or so they claimed), as the divine prophets had foretold these and ten thousand other wonderful things concerning him, and the tribe of Christians, so named from him, are not extinct at this day.

John Davidson, in his *Gospel of Jesus*, asserts that most scholars today think that there has indeed been some tampering with the original words of Josephus in later Christian editions of his works, and he gives us what he considers to be the more probable rendering:

At about this time lived Jesus, a wise man. He performed astonishing feats and was a teacher of such people as are eager for novelties. He attracted many Jews and many of the Greeks. His followers claimed that he was the Messiah. Upon an indictment brought by leading men of our society, Pilate condemned him to the cross, but those who had loved him from the first did not cease to be attracted to him. According to their story, on the third day he appeared to them, restored to life, as, they say, the holy prophets had foretold. The brotherhood of the Christians named after him, is still in existence to this day.

Certainly an amended version is more likely. All right, so Josephus was not to be taken in by fairy tales, and most people would agree that he would have given a sound account of the facts as he understood them. The point I would make is that he never denied that Jesus was one of those facts. He was a historian, not a story-teller, and if he had not believed that Jesus existed, he would have said: '*There was a story going round among the people* about this time...' That time was so close to his own, many of his readers would have known if his report was based on a fabrication.

A very brief mention of Jesus can also be found in the writings of Gaius Cornelius Tacitus (AD 55–120) and Gaius Suetonius Tranquillus (AD 75–160), both of them trustworthy Roman historians. Suetonius tells us that there were so many Jews in Rome at the time of the Emperor Claudius (AD 41–54), 'stirred up by one Christus', that the Emperor had gone so far as to banish them from the city. And we learn from Tacitus that things were no better in AD 64, at the time of the great fire. He has nothing good to say of Jesus, or of his followers:

They (the Christians) got their name from Christus, who received the death penalty in the reign of Tiberius, by sentence of the procurator Pontius Pilate. That checked the pernicious superstition for

32

a short time, but it broke out afresh – not only in Judaea, where the plague first arose, but in the capital itself (Rome), where all things horrible and shameful in the world collect and find a home.

But Tacitus obviously believed that those crazed followers of Christus had a real man to follow.

And later, in AD 105, Pliny the Younger, the governor of Bithynia, wrote to the Emperor Trajan that all the temples had been deserted for a long time because there were so many of those Christians. Though he did admit that their conduct gave no cause for complaint. And certainly he did not suggest that they were followers of a dream-figure.

One would not expect much information about Jesus from men like these. Why should they bother with him? All over the Empire there were other leaders of other sects, many of them claiming to be the Messiah; and what they said, or what they did, provided that it was no threat to Rome, was no great concern of theirs. But, living as they did so soon after the death of Jesus, they would almost certainly have known of him, or known of some persons who had known him, or seen him, in his lifetime; and so the question of his having had a lifetime did not arise. And surely Pliny the Elder would have told his nephew something pertinent about Jesus if he had thought it of any great import. As he would have told him to cancel out any mention of him if he had not existed.

However much of the story about Jesus may not be true in a historical sense, it has always fascinated many people, even those of other religions. Muhammad (Mohammed, Mahomet), the founder of Islam, has nothing but a good word to say of Jesus the man, although he shows less interest in the Jesus of myth,

33

and of course he does not accept that Jesus is greater than he is! But certainly Muhammad was more realistic. Right from the start he insisted that he, Muhammad, was not God, and his followers must not believe any such thing. He wanted to ensure that he would come down in history as a genuine Master and not an impostor; as a real man and not a myth – unlike the Buddha and Jesus.

Jesus could not have heard of Muhammad, who came after him (AD 570–632), but he most probably would have known something of the Buddha (Gautama Siddhartha), an Indian prince and the founder of Buddhism, for Asoka, the Emperor of India, had sent out missionaries as far as Alexandria, and other towns of the Middle East, to preach the message of the Buddha to all who had not heard of this God-man and his transcendent wisdom. But Gautama lived from around 563 BC so he could not have known anything of Jesus Christ. If he had lived in Jesus' time, and had heard of him, he would almost certainly have had something to say about him, as did Muhammad. But just as his message and that of Muhammad have lived on, so has that of Jesus, even if that message has all along been interpreted by his followers as it suits them.

To give just one instance: Jesus taught that we should love our enemies, and if anyone strikes us on the cheek, we should turn to him the other cheek. But no government of any country has ever taken him seriously on that point. And it could be argued that no government should. For Jesus himself can be guilty of inconsistency at times. When he goes charging into the temple, hurling abuse at the moneychangers, and leaves the whole place a total wreck, he makes a poor show of loving his enemies. People could be forgiven for saying, 'If he can't practise what he preaches, why should we listen

34

to his preaching?' And indeed, though the Church in every Christian country has upheld its firm belief in the God-man Jesus, people everywhere have always had their own opinions about him.

As well as the writers I have already mentioned, there is another I should not forget. David Friedrich Strauss, a nineteenth century German theologian, is known for his *Life of Jesus*, in which he endeavours to show that the whole Jesus story is myth, and some other theologians were in agreement with him. In an earlier age they would not have lived to tell the tale, let alone carry on in their profession, but this was a more tolerant age, and some of those who read Strauss's book even went further and maintained that Jesus never existed. For by then that theory was already a subject of investigation among scholars.

Today, in America, the scholars of the Jesus Seminar, having made a close study of all the relevant literature available, have concluded that, although Jesus has so much of the mythical about him, he was in fact a real man. They do not take as truth the virgin birth story, and they are not prepared to believe in Jesus' miraculous powers, although they do accept that he could have healed certain psychosomatic ailments. And of course they don't believe in Jesus' resurrection. They hold that Paul was responsible for that story, along with Peter and Mary Magdalene. They do not believe the impossible, but they are willing to accept the highly improbable. Their Jesus is a man, but he is quite unlike all other men. He does not share with them their manifold imperfections. He is, you could say, much too good to be true! Certainly those men of the Seminar are deserving of our respect, but it could be said that in taking such a rational stance (for the most part) they fail to grasp the real meaning which, according to other equally rational people, lies behind the myth. And that is true, but at least they are right, as I see it, in believing that Jesus did exist. He was a real man; that, I repeat, is the truth. But the myth that has been built up around him is every bit as true, and just as it originally belonged to Iusu (Horus), so it belongs to Jesus.

But in support of the opposing point of view I did find much of very great interest in *The Gospel of Jesus* by John Davidson. Instead of making a blunt, and, surely, absurd denial that Jesus ever existed, he makes a noble attempt to reveal the God-man in his true light. The man existed, but he was no mortal man. He was, Davidson claims, a Master, one of many who had come before him, and will come after. A Master is the Logos, the Word of God made flesh, a seeming mortal who has chosen to abandon his blessed state of being one with God in order to track down as many sinful souls as will pay heed to his teaching, and permit him to guide them along the path of righteousness to that blessed state which was his before he put on his garment of flesh so that he could speak to them as man to man.

What I would say to John Davidson is this: If Jesus knew he was a Master, the incarnate Word, come into the world to bring all those who would listen to him to his Father, then why did he wait until he was thirty years old to get started? Especially if he knew, as the Bible tells us, that he had only three years to go. And if he was really all he professed to be (according to this submission), how is it that he was so sure that the end of the world was imminent? Time has proved him wrong, as also in another case. We learn from The Dialogue of the Saviour, a Coptic codex discovered in Egypt near the town of Nag Hammâdi, that Jesus said this: 'The earth does not move. If it were to move, it would fall'. And surely common sense would show

36

much else that he is supposed to have said about himself to be wrong too. Though there is no proof that he ever said the half of it, and it may well be that almost everything he *actually* said was true, and its meaning is clear to any intelligent person. However, it must be admitted that much of what he had to say was of a mystical nature, as has been made perfectly plain by the ancient manuscripts that have been discovered in Egypt, especially the Nag Hammâdi codices, unearthed in 1945. If these had not been found we should not have the Gospel of Thomas with the new light it throws on the sayings of Jesus.

The apostle Thomas, Didymos (the twin) Judas Thomas, had been close to his Master throughout his ministry (though for him 'Master' probably had a different meaning from the one Davidson gives it), and would have been familiar with his sayings. And indeed many of those sayings reported by him do bear a close resemblance to those recounted in the canonical Gospels. Nevertheless, there is a difference. It is obvious that Thomas was a confirmed Gnostic, as his Master may well have been too. But Jesus' teaching is not just for Gnostics. It is not veiled in obscurity. For the most part, what he says is clear to anyone and straight to the point. I cannot see him standing up before a crowd of ordinary Jews, saying this sort of thing:

Happy is he who already was before he is.

Or this:

When you make eyes in place of an eye, and a hand in place of a hand, and a foot in place of a foot, and an image in place of an image, then shall you enter the Kingdom.

37

Or: Become yourselves, passing away!

Or: When you bring forth that in yourselves, this which is yours will save you; if you do not have that in yourselves, this which is not yours in you will kill you.

Or: The angels with the prophets will come to you and they will give you what is yours. You also, what is in your hands give that to them, and say to yourselves: On which day will they come and receive what is theirs?

Or: He who knows the Father and the Mother, will he be called the son of a harlot?

Or: Woe to the flesh that depends upon the soul! Woe to the soul that depends upon the flesh!

Or: Blessed is the lion which the man eats, and the lion will become man; and cursed is the man whom the lion eats, and the lion will become man.

Or: It is rightly said: The inner, the outer, and what is outside the outer.

Long before he was done, his audience would have walked off and left him to it. All that is *like* what Jesus said, but it is not *how* he said it.

No. That was not Jesus' style at all. What he had to say seemed to him to be of the utmost importance, and he wanted to be sure that all his listeners understood it. And so his usual way of getting his message across was by speaking to them in parables, which were far from being esoteric sayings with a secret meaning; they were simple tales with simple parallels to everyday experience, which anyone with a normal degree of intelligence would have no difficulty in understanding. And just in case any of them did, he was always ready with an explanation.

Here is just one of his many parables as Mark gives it:

> In his teaching he said to them: 'Listen! A sower went out to sow. And as he sowed, some seed fell along the path, and the birds came and devoured it. Other seed fell on rocky ground, where there was not much soil, and immediately, since it had no depth of soil, the first shoots appeared, but when the sun rose they were scorched, and since they had no roots they withered away. Other seed fell among thorns and the thorns grew up and choked the shoots, and they yielded no grain. And other seeds fell into good soil and brought forth grain, growing up and increasing and yielding thirtyfold and sixtyfold and a hundredfold.' And he said, 'He who has ears to hear, let him hear.'

> Mark 4: 3–9

And here is his explanation:

> 'The sower sows the word. And these are the ones along the path, where the word is sown; when they hear, Satan immediately comes and takes away the word which is sown in them. And these in like manner are the ones sown upon rocky ground, who, when they hear the word, immediately receive it with joy; but having no root in themselves, they endure for a while; then,

when tribulation or persecution arises on account
of the word, immediately they fall away. And others
are the ones sown among thorns; they are those
who hear the word, but the cares of the world,
and the delight in riches, and the desire for other
things, enter in and choke the word, and it proves
unfruitful. But those that were sown upon the good
soil are the ones who hear the word and accept it,
they bear fruit thirtyfold and sixtyfold and a
hundredfold.'

Mark 4: 14–20

That one may not be the easiest of his parables to
understand completely without some help, but the general
idea is plain enough, and certainly there is nothing there
to appeal to Gnostics.

Jesus must have realized that the doctrine of the
Logos – the Word made flesh – was no new concept.
The Egyptians had taught it centuries before, as a reality
applying not just to any special person, but to all of
us. We are all a part of the one God. Many of the
Greeks, especially those who were adherents of Orphism,
(a mystic religion in ancient Greece as early as the
seventh or sixth centuries BC), and all those who were
in agreement with Pythagoras and Plato, held the same
belief, as did the devotees of all the Mystery religions
of antiquity. The difference between a Master and an
ordinary man is that the Master has more than just a
glimmer of the divine essence in him. He is himself
the very God incarnate.

The problem I have with this is the same problem I
have been dealing with all along. As John Davidson
explains, God is the Father of all, and the Logos, the
Word, is the creative power emanating from Him, his

very Son in fact. And that Son, being God in the flesh, is the Master. The Word in itself is the Holy Ghost. And together they form the Trinity, three aspects of the one God. Yet this Master, this Son of God, could not give a satisfactory answer to his disciples' question as to the time of the end of the world. So was he really all he claimed to be?

The Jews, of course – most of them – were not to be persuaded, and certainly they did see Jesus as a real man. In their Talmud it is stated that in the reign of Tiberius a sorcerer called Jesus, who claimed to be the Son of God, had been hanged for his vicious onslaught on the Jewish faith. There is no suggestion that the Christians had made up this story. That man was *there* all right.

But perhaps the most convincing evidence is provided by the Gospels. If the myth-makers had wanted to present Jesus as the Word made flesh, the very Son of God, who had *chosen* to die on the cross in order to save mankind, would they have had him cry out in his last moments, 'My God, my God! [this to his *father]* Why have you forsaken me?' ('Why have you left me to this cruel fate I never asked for and have not deserved?') I hardly think so.

And would they ever have allowed him to speak to his mother – holy Mary, mother of God – in the way he did?

'What have I to do with you, woman?'

John 2: 4

The Bible says that Jesus claimed to be the Son of God, and at times it would appear that he even went further:

41

'I and the Father are one.'

John 1: 30

And:

'He who has seen me has seen the Father.'

John 14: 9

Yet in Mark's Gospel, when a man addresses him as 'Good master', Jesus will have none of it. 'Why do you call me good?' he is reported to have said. 'No one is good but God alone.' Mark 10: 18

And in John's Gospel he says (obviously to dispel any delusions that people might be labouring under) 'The Father is greater than I.' John 14: 28

This is not in accord with his contrary claim, 'I and the Father are one', and it is not in accord with the myth.

And, moreover, would the myth-makers have chosen a prostitute for their God-man's sweetheart? Or, supposing that was their intention, would they not have called her by her name instead of mysteriously referring to her as 'the beloved disciple'? Or, if that disciple was someone else, why not tell us who it was?

In their book *The Laughing Jesus* Timothy Freke and Peter Gandy declare that the Scriptures are 'full of crap'. The whole story of Jesus is nothing but a myth. But really such a myth would be full of flaws, as I hope the evidence I have given has demonstrated. It is just because Jesus did actually exist that the 'true' and the 'untrue' can lie side by side together. The myth is not good enough to cover up the stark reality.

Of course most of the stuff told about Jesus is pure myth, but a myth is not a lie. It is a marvellous metaphor concealing a great truth beyond our comprehension. This myth has been built up around the true man by those admirers who expected more of him, and all those who came after him who are always looking for wonders. But some of them, at least, may have understood the true meaning behind the myth. As Joseph Campbell so aptly puts it, 'Myth is what never was, yet always is'.

But just because the myth about Jesus is a great truth, that cannot mean, to turn that statement round, that the truth is a lie. That is a contradiction in terms, and it would be saying that a myth is a lie. The man Jesus is as true as the myth, and we should never lose sight of him.

2

So, if Jesus did exist, what sort of man was he?

Was he good-looking? – Beauty comes from within, and on that account I think he was more than just good-looking; he must have been beautiful. It is plain that he was a good mixer, of a cheerful and friendly disposition, one of those people in fact who habitually gather a crowd around them. And to anyone who has thought about his teachings, and the meaning of the parables he employed, it must be evident that he was highly intelligent. Though I confess that in this regard I do have my reservations. I call to mind the incident described as *the cleansing of the temple*:

> And Jesus entered the temple of God and drove out all who sold and bought in the temple, and he overturned the tables of the moneychangers, and the seats of those who sold pigeons. He said to them 'It is written, "My house shall be called a house of prayer", but you make it a den of robbers.'

> Matthew 21: 12

Jesus was an outspoken character, and that is as it should be. He could *say* whatever he thought, but if he wanted to get a point across he was going the wrong way about it. He knew perfectly well that he had to be on his guard at all times when dealing with the likes of the temple authorities, so why did he go out of his way to upset them? And, as well, I am of the opinion that to lose one's temper is never an intelligent response to any provocation; and Jesus quite clearly lost his in this instance.

And then there is his attitude towards Gentiles. At times, in spite of the doctrine of love he preached, he showed no love for anyone who did not happen to be a Jew, as the following quotation makes very clear:

> A certain woman whose young daughter was possessed by an unclean spirit, heard of him, and came and fell down at his feet. Now the woman was a Greek, a Syrophoenician by birth. And she begged him to cast the demon out of her daughter. And he said to her, 'Let the children first be fed, for it is not right to take the children's bread and throw it to the dogs.' [Here, of course, 'the children' are the children of Israel, and 'the dogs' are the Gentiles.]

Mark 7: 27

I should find it hard to believe that Jesus said that, if the 'bitch' he was addressing had not believed it herself. But I have to say this does not strike me as a particularly intelligent utterance. It is one typical of those today who flauntingly style themselves 'Brits', or 'Aussies', or what not. But as I see it, all patriotism is foolishness. Whether you are British, Australian, American, French, German, Greek, Italian, Spanish, Dutch, Russian, Indian, African, Chinese, Japanese, or any other, it makes no difference. Or whether you are a Jew, a Christian, a Muslim, a Hindu, a Buddhist, a Sufi, a Parsee, or any other. Which country you happen

46

to live in, or to have been born in, is of no greater consequence than in which street your house stands; and although people everywhere have always found their differences of religious belief harder to accept, the same applies there. It is not where you live, or what you believe, it is what sort of person you are that matters. And one would think that Jesus would not have needed to be told that.

The plain fact is, Jesus was not all that different from other adherents of a particular faith, and like many British nationals not so long ago, who were in the habit of calling black people 'niggers', he was, like any other Jew of his time, intolerant of 'Gentiles'. But he did have a change of heart. Mark continues with the story:

But she answered him, 'Yes, Lord; yet even the dogs under the table eat the children's crumbs.' And he said to her, 'For this saying you may go your way; the demon has left your daughter.' And she went home, and found the child lying in bed, and the demon gone.

Mark 28: 30

Even so, Jesus took his time to see things the way that woman did.

Matthew gives us another instance of Jesus' attitude to Gentiles, this time changed for the better:

As he entered Capernaum, a centurion came forward to him, beseeching him and saying, 'Lord, my servant is lying paralysed at home, in terrible distress.' And he said to him, 'I will come and heal him.' But the centurion answered him, 'Lord, I am not worthy to have you come under my roof;

47

but only say the word, and my servant will be healed. For I am a man under authority, with soldiers under me; and I say to one, "Go", and he goes, and to another "Come", and he comes, and to my slave, "Do this", and he does it.' When Jesus heard him, he marvelled, and said to those who followed him, 'Truly, I say to you, not even in Israel have I found such faith. I tell you, many will come from east and west and sit at table with Abraham, Isaac, and Jacob in the kingdom of heaven, while the sons of the kingdom will be thrown into the outer darkness; there men will weep and gnash their teeth.' And to the centurion Jesus said, 'Go, be it done for you as you have believed.' And the servant was healed at that very moment.

Matthew 8: 5–13

So Jesus could be made to see reason. But surely a man of such great intelligence should not have required a Syrophoenician woman or a Roman centurion to win him over.

But did he learn his lesson all that well? Matthew goes on to tell us that after he had chosen his twelve apostles and given them a share of his own miraculous powers, he sent them out as 'labourers into his harvest', to preach to all the people, and gave them these instructions:

'Go nowhere among the Gentiles, and enter no town of the Samaritans, but go rather to the lost sheep of the house of Israel.'

Matthew 10: 5–6

48

Evidence, I think, that Jesus was not all he is made out to be. But he could be persuaded. And in the main he was certainly a highly intelligent man. And a very charismatic one. If he had not been that, he would never have attracted such a considerable following.

But even so, if it had not been for St Paul, his message might well have ended up, more or less, a dead duck. Paul did not stop at feeding the 'children'; he set out to win over the Gentiles, and his great success was due to his conviction and his perseverance. Jesus had something more to offer. His charisma. And that won him more than just numbers. It attracted all sorts of interesting and diverse individuals, among whom was a prostitute.

Mary of Magdala, Mary Magdalene, has been accounted one of Jesus' disciples, but I would not call her that. She followed him around, certainly, and I think she may have had her reasons, quite apart from any interest she would undoubtedly have had in his teachings. It has been suggested that she was his sweetheart, or even his wife; but if that were true, why make such a secret of it?

Philip, one of Jesus' apostles, makes no secret of it. Dan Brown, the author of *The Da Vinci Code*, gives us this quote from his Gospel:

And the companion of the Saviour is Mary Magdalene. Christ loved her more than all the disciples and used to kiss her often on her mouth. The rest of the disciples were offended by it and expressed disapproval. They said to him, 'Why do you love her more than all of us?'

What more proof could you ask for? If it is true. But here 'mouth' could be a mistranslation, for while

49

it is usual to say 'on the cheek' or 'on the forehead', a kiss on the mouth is normally just called a kiss; and, moreover, if Mary was Jesus' wife, or even just his girlfriend, would his disciples have held out for their fair share of his love?

If we are to believe the joint authors of *The Holy Blood and the Holy Grail* – Michael Baigent, Richard Leigh, and Henry Lincoln – Mary Magdalene had very little to do with Jesus; she was physically and spiritually linked with John the Baptist who, they claim, could well have been the Lord we would venerate as John Christ if the followers of his rival, Jesus, had not wanted it their way and put John in a subordinate place.

But whatever the facts of the matter may be, facts are not my chief concern. I seek the truth that lies behind the personalities of the Jesus and Mary of the Gospels, and fact is not quite the same as truth. Indeed there is nothing – or almost nothing – you can't 'prove' to be true if you put your mind to it. Jesus can be anything from a self-interested magician to God's own Son, and Mary Magdalene can be a common whore or a goddess of wisdom and light. Dan Brown's proof-hunt has made his book a best-seller, though it has to be said that it is more than that. The author has something to tell us worth telling, something which the common reader, as opposed to the scholar, can readily take in. Having made a study of the life and works of Leonardo da Vinci, he holds that the disciple sitting next to Jesus in his famous painting of the Last Supper – the one leaning across Jesus' breast – was really, originally, a woman, Mary Magdalene. But whatever Leonardo may have chosen to think, or Dan Brown, St John the Evangelist tells us plainly that on this same occasion, after Jesus had confided to the disciples that one of them sitting at the table with him would betray him,

One of his disciples, whom Jesus loved, was lying close to the breast of Jesus, so Simon Peter beckoned to him and said, 'Tell us who it is of whom he speaks'.

John 13: 23–24

Simon Peter was addressing *him*: no woman.

There have been differing postulates put forward as to where Mary fits into the picture. At times she has been taken out of her sordid milieu and transformed into some sort of mystical figure. But I hardly see Mary Magdalene as any sort of stand-in for Hagia Sophia (Sacred Wisdom). If she had been so wise, would she have given herself reason to repent? But if she is not the right woman for the job the makers of the myth are reputed (by some) to have given her, she does make a suitable companion for a man like Jesus. She was a real woman just as he was a real man. And besides, the female goddess who is eligible for a place in the story would surely be Jesus' mother. For, although Jesus himself in his life was relatively distant from her, she is the star of the original myth – the myth that began before Jesus' birth, and she has held almost equal rank with him ever since his death. Even in the Nicene Creed she is given an honourable place:

For us men and for our salvation he came down from heaven and was incarnate by the Holy Ghost of the Virgin Mary, and was made man.

Right from birth this 'pure virgin's' whole life verged on the miraculous. She grew up in the Temple of the Lord where she was 'nurtured like a dove and received food from the hand of an angel' (Protevangelium Jacobi), and on her death she was carried bodily by angels up to heaven to reign there as their Queen.

Mary Magdalene had almost faded out of the picture until the authors of *The Holy Blood and the Holy Grail* dug her out again, and Lynn Picknett and Clive Prince followed up with their compelling book *The Templar Revelation*, and then Dan Brown put Mary well and truly in the spotlight. But she played only a small part in Jesus' story, and no part in the original myth. She is a historical personage who has been made use of by recent writers wishing to improve upon the myth.

The point is – and it is a point that must be noted – she is the one prominent female follower of Jesus. Certain other women get a mention, but Mary's role is one of enough significance for some to accord her the title of 'disciple', although, as I have already said, I would not so describe her. And certainly, for all her closeness to Jesus, she was not chosen to be one of his twelve apostles. (But then, Jesus, as a man of his time, would not have considered any woman to be suitable for that job.)

If she was a prostitute (and we can not be certain that she was) I doubt if that would have worried Jesus all that much. The way others saw 'sin' was not the way he saw it. She was as free as anyone else to keep him company. And it would appear that she was a definite member of his immediate circle, although Jesus himself, so far as I can see, paid no special attention to her.

He may have been not a little flattered by the attention she paid him, and certainly, if she was a prostitute and still practising her trade, or even just living off the proceeds of her past pursuit, her money would have stood him in good stead from time to time. Not everyone would have kept an open purse for him.

Although, apparently, Mary's was not the only purse at his disposal, for Luke gives us this interesting information:

He went on through the cities and villages, preaching and bringing the good news of the kingdom of God. And the twelve were with him, and also some who had been healed of evil spirits and infirmities: Mary, called Magdalene, from whom seven demons had gone out, and Joanna, the wife of Chuza, Herod's steward, and Susanna, and many others, who provided for them out of their means.

Luke 8: 1–3

It looks as though Mary Magdalene may not have been the only prostitute in Jesus' entourage. But they weren't the only ones he depended on. In Matthew's Gospel, before his apostles are to set out on their preaching mission, Jesus gives them these instructions:

'Carry no purse, no bag, no sandals; and salute no one on the road. Whatever house you enter, first say, "Peace be to this house!" And if a son of peace is there, your peace shall rest upon him; but if not, it shall return to you. And remain in the same house, eating and drinking what they provide, for the labourer deserves his wages; do not go from house to house. Whenever you enter a town and they receive you, eat what is set before you; heal the sick in it and say to them, "The kingdom of God has come near to you." But whenever you enter a town and they do not receive you, go into the streets and say, "Even the dust of your town that clings to our feet, we wipe off against you!"'

Matthew 10: 9–14

Not very gracious, I must say. And if Jesus could

53

see no good reason why he or his apostles should earn their living in the ordinary way, I don't need to tell you how he would be described today.

But today is not yesterday, and it would appear that he got away with it. Jesus was indeed a very persuasive character, and, I would say, on the whole a happy one, the sort that usually finds an open door wherever he goes. Until his tragic end came he had no reason not to be happy. Although he had no job he wanted for nothing. He knew what it was to dine with the best. From the first there was always a table in wait for him, and a bed made ready for him at the end of the day, and at the last, when he was hanging on the cross, the soldiers standing round cast lots for his tunic. John gives us the best account:

> When the soldiers had crucified Jesus they took his garments and made four parts, one for each soldier, also his tunic. But the tunic was without seam, woven from top to bottom; so they said to one another, 'Let us not tear it, but cast lots for it to see whose it shall be.'

> John 19: 23–24

So it must have been worth something. Why else would they have had their eyes on it? The man hanging on the cross meant nothing to them. His tunic would hardly rank with Elvis Presley's waistcoat!

Apparently Jesus had a point when he said, 'The labourer deserves his wages.'

But St Paul did not hold with that, and the fact that he said so is clear evidence that he didn't always agree with Jesus. In his Second Letter to the Thessalonians he says:

We did not eat anyone's bread without paying.

2 Thessalonians 3: 8

And:

If anyone will not work, let him not eat.

2 Thessalonians 3: 10

To judge by the instructions Jesus gave to his apostles when he sent them out on their preaching mission, it is plain that he must have known what it was to be turned away at times. (Not surprising, if he had no job.) But there was always Mary.

Though Mary's reasons for being on hand were not entirely charitable. I do believe she was in love with Jesus. Those who are of the opinion that it was the other way round have got it wrong.

Jesus was most probably attractive physically (as well as in other ways), and any intelligent woman would have given him a second look. He did not appear to have a girlfriend in tow, and Mary, probably herself a good-looking and intelligent woman, and a passionate one, very soon fell hopelessly in love with him.

Jesus must have known how she felt about him, and I believe that he was genuinely fond of her, but he could not return her love in the way she wanted. Jesus was a homosexual.

And I shall never cease to be amazed that so many people have failed to realize that.

If I were to point out to you a particular young man, and I said to you, 'Take a look at that one over there; he's the chap that Robert loves,' what conclusion would you come to regarding Robert?

55

You might answer, 'Yes, but you are calling him a "chap".' I am. I call a spade a spade; unlike the Church whose practice is anything but above-board. For years it has gone out of its way to delude us.

But if the 'chap' I pointed to was parading about in drag, would you be deluded?

The Church intends that you should. The sex of the 'beloved disciple' has been kept a dark secret at all times. Or it is never openly admitted. (Although Irenaeus, a zealous man of the Church, always maintained that the beloved disciple was John. But most probably he did not imagine that Jesus' love for him was of a sexual nature). And the party in opposition – the Jews – would have gone along with the Church's policy, for a homosexual was not a description they would have been willing to accept as appertaining to any one of them.

The fact is, until recent times homosexuality has been frowned upon by the Church and by governments everywhere, and Jesus, as a Jew of his times, would have understood their way of looking at things; though certainly he did his best to take a more reasonable stance. For instance, when he said:

'There are eunuchs who have been so from birth, and there are eunuchs who have been made eunuchs by men, and there are eunuchs who have made themselves eunuchs for the sake of the kingdom of heaven',

and then:

'He who is able to receive it, let him receive it',

Matthew 19: 12

56

he could hardly have expressed his own view more aptly, or more sympathetically, if reservedly. But the original discussion he was holding was about marriage and adultery. Jesus himself turned the subject round from the point, or lack of it, of the marriage ceremony, to the rights, or wrongs, of homosexual practice. And he could have been justifying his own position. Or he could have been leaving it open to question.

At this point I must acknowledge my indebtedness to Ian Wilson, the author of *Jesus – The Evidence*, for his exposition of certain excerpts from the Secret Gospel of Thomas. He points out that Jesus had a 'strikingly modern attitude to nudity'. (I don't agree with Wilson here. This is just another instance of the odd belief that we 'moderns' are in every way superior to the people who lived long before our time; a belief which is just as silly as the belief that we are superior to people who were born in another country. Very few people today would wish to be seen naked even in their own home, except by their sexual partner. Jesus was just one of those men of any time who have no problem with nudity.)

Wilson quotes Thomas:

His disciples said 'When will you be revealed to us and when shall we see you?' Jesus said 'When you disrobe without being ashamed and take up your garments and place them under your feet like little children, and tread on them...'

Wilson goes on to refer to a letter discovered by Dr Morton Smith, a Columbia University professor, which appeared to be a copy of an earlier letter written by Clement of Alexandria, a Church Father of the second century AD. This letter tells of a secret gospel of Mark which contains some interesting information not included

57

in any of the canonical Gospels. For when the men of the Church went sorting through all the original manuscripts, they retained what they liked and discarded what they didn't, and obviously they felt that what they found in this Gospel, while it could not be false, was beyond the ability of the average decent churchgoer to understand.

And now, see what you understand from this quotation from the Secret Gospel:

And they came into Bethany, and a certain woman, whose brother had died, [probably Lazarus] was there. And, coming, she prostrated herself before Jesus and says to him, 'Son of David, have mercy on me.' But the disciples rebuked her. And Jesus, being angered, went off with her into the garden where the tomb was, and straightway a great cry was heard from the tomb. And going near, Jesus rolled away the stone from the door of the tomb. And straightway, going in where the youth was, he stretched forth his hand and raised him, seizing his hand. But the youth, looking upon him, loved him and began to beseech him that he might be with him. And going out of the tomb they came into the house of the youth, for he was rich. And after six days Jesus told him what to do and in the evening the youth comes to him, wearing a linen cloth over [his] naked [body]. And he remained with him that night, for Jesus taught him the mystery of the kingdom of God. And thence, arising, he returned to the other side of the Jordan.

Of course you may conclude that the two of them spent the night discussing spiritual matters. Think what you will.

And then Wilson goes on to give us this further information:

He [Clement of Alexandria] also fills in what is an otherwise unexplained gap in verse 46 of the tenth chapter of the canonical Mark Gospel: 'They reached Jericho, and as he left Jericho...'

'For centuries,' says Wilson, 'scholars have puzzled over what might have happened in Jericho.' According to the Clement letter, the Secret Gospel originally read:

And the sister of the youth whom Jesus loved and his mother and Salome, were there, and Jesus did not receive them.

And there is this, from the canonical Mark Gospel:

A young man who followed him (at the time of Jesus' arrest in Gethsemane) had nothing on but a linen cloth; they caught hold of him, but he left the cloth in their hands and ran away naked.

Mark 14: 51–52

Surely it must appear to any impartial reader that the Secret Gospel was saying more about Jesus than the canonical Gospel was prepared to admit. And it could well be that that youth was the 'beloved disciple'.

Jesus knew how it stood with him, of course, and it is most likely that his mother had early on made an intelligent guess as to what type of man her son was sexually. And his close friends would have known. Only Mary remained in the dark. Many years ago I was in the same situation as Mary, so I can tell you, she would not have wanted to know. She just carried on living in hopes, given every encouragement, no doubt, by all those kisses his disciples complained of (according to the apostle Philip). Jesus must have realized how much she suffered. He would have done better to have come clean with her. Any homosexual man in his position would naturally find it difficult to do that, and apparently Jesus was no exception. In this respect. But from an early age there was, unblinking, his difference staring back at him. A Jewish boy was normally expected to marry and raise a family, but Jesus, as he grew older, must have realized that this was not for him. The neighbours were giving him funny looks, and his mother was showing increasing uneasiness.

He never had anything to say about his mother, and certainly he cannot be held responsible for all the nonsense that has been written about her. He does not appear to have had any great love for either her or Joseph, not because they were not good parents, but because he felt he had nothing in common with them. And since he had no intention of working as a carpenter at the bench beside his father for the rest of his life, as soon as he could get away from them both, he did. He may have joined some religious fraternity such as the Nazarenes or the Essenes, and there he may have met up with the one he loved who was probably the apostle John. Whether he was the same youth he is supposed to have raised from the dead, we cannot know, but judging by what we do know, he was very close to Jesus. And interestingly, we learn from a Coptic codex found at Nag Hammâdi, the Pistis Sophia, that Jesus referred to the apostle John as 'John the maiden'. Hardly suitable for inclusion in the Gospel story!

Whatever Jesus' sexual inclination may have been, there was more to him than that, and he knew it. When he reached the age of thirty (according to the myth, though it was more probably earlier) he took a good hard look at himself, and if the brotherhood had brought him any significant benefits, he was beginning to feel that enough was enough. If he was ever to make anything of his life he had better make a start.

He was mindful of his cousin (his second cousin) John, who had already made a name for himself. People called him 'the Baptizer'.

In those days came John the Baptist, preaching in the wilderness of Judaea, and saying,
'Repent, for the kingdom of heaven is at hand.'

Matthew 3: 1–2

And the Gospel goes on to say:

For this is he who was spoken of by the prophet Isaiah when he said, 'The voice of one crying in the wilderness: "Prepare the way of the Lord, make his paths straight."'

Now John wore a garment of camel's hair and a leather girdle around his waist; and his food was locusts and wild honey. Then went out to him Jerusalem and all Judaea and all the regions about the Jordan, and they were baptized by him in the river Jordan, confessing their sins.

But when he saw many of the Pharisees and Sadducees coming for baptism, he said to them, 'You brood of vipers! Who warned you to flee from the wrath to come? Bear fruit that befits repentance, and do not presume to say to yourselves, "We have Abraham as our father"; for I tell you, God is able from these stones to raise up children

61

to Abraham. Even now the axe is laid to the root of the trees; every tree therefore that does not bear good fruit is cut down and thrown into the fire.

I baptize you with water for repentance, but he who is coming after me is mightier than I, whose sandals I am not worthy to carry; he will baptize you with the Holy Spirit and with fire. His winnowing fork is in his hand, and he will clear his threshing floor and gather his wheat into the granary, but the chaff he will burn with unquenchable fire.'

Matthew 3: 1–12

No doubt Jesus would have heard a good deal about his cousin's doings, and that talk of the one who was to come must have set him wondering. The food that went into John's mouth would not have appealed to Jesus, but the words that came out of it held a great fascination for him. He went down to the Jordan and sought out his cousin and asked to be baptized by him. But John demurred:

'I need to be baptized by you, and do you come to me?'

Matthew 3: 14

Jesus does not seem to have been at all taken aback by John's response, so it does look as if he had indeed given some thought to his cousin's talk of the one who was to come. And, according to the Bible, the conclusion he arrived at was the right one. For, it is stated, when Jesus came up out of the water,

Behold, the heavens were opened and he saw the Spirit of God descending like a dove, and alighting on him; and lo, a voice from heaven, saying, 'This is my beloved Son, with whom I am well pleased.'

Matthew 3: 16–17

From its very beginning this story can not have been anything but a myth (though the baptism itself would have been a fact). And I am not thinking just of the voice from heaven. John went on preaching and baptizing after the baptism of Jesus, and so it doesn't look as though he was prepared to hand the job over to a better man. And, moreover, he could not have known that Jesus was the coming one he was speaking of, and if he did, why didn't he go and seek *him* out long before he reached the age of thirty?

But this is the unlikely story we are asked to believe: John was a well-known teacher and baptizer. His cousin went down to the Jordan to be baptized by him. John didn't want to do it as he knew that it should be the other way round. And the voice from heaven said 'aye aye'.

And after that Jesus went his own way. First, for forty days, he was in the wilderness, 'to be tempted by the devil', and having stood up against the wiles of Satan, he was ready to set out on his mission.

But when he heard that John had been imprisoned by King Herod, he must have realized that his own time was limited. In the three years left to him he spent his whole time preaching to the people, and he gave his twelve apostles instructions as to how they should go about their preaching after he was gone. He is reputed to have performed countless miracles (only just over thirty have been recorded), some of which can be explained, while others are beyond the credence of any sane person. And even more incredible is the story that he gave his apostles the same miraculous power to perform wonders. In fact, although none of the canonical Gospels give us an account of any miracle performed by them, we learn from Acts, and from many of the Apocryphal writings, that the apostles outdid Jesus. One of them even raised a sardine from the dead! It would hardly have required a very clever conjurer to tackle that one.

It is the miracles of Jesus, as much as those of his apostles, that have all along given readers of the Gospels the greatest cause for concern. They cannot be true. As about many other matters, John Davidson has something very interesting to say on this subject:

> Perhaps the point of greatest significance in a study of these miracles is that practically all of them, whether in St John or in the synoptics, are also used by the metaphysical writers of the time – and often by Jesus, too – as metaphors for spiritual truths. We are all spiritually blind, deaf and dumb. We are crippled and have forgotten how to walk straight in this world. We are carrying a heavy burden of weaknesses and sins from which we need to be healed. Our will power is paralysed and withered by our attention to the world of the senses. In fact, we have become spiritually dead and full of darkness – we need to be raised from the dead, to come out of the tomb of the body, not after four days but after many ages. Spiritually, we 'stinketh' with the accumulated sins of many lifetimes!
>
> To accomplish this, we need a spiritual physician to help us to overcome the feverish activities of

the mind, to learn how to walk upon the stormy waters of this world, to cast out the devils and demons of human weakness from within ourselves and to overcome the Devil himself. With the help of a Son of God, we must bathe in the pool of Living Water and come up healed after many years of infirmity without anyone having previously helped us to take that dip. We need to eat the true Bread of Life and to drink the wine of divine love at the marriage of the soul with God.

Well, I can find no fault with that interpretation, and it is deserving of our serious consideration. But even so, I am not in complete agreement with Davidson. I do believe that the reader of the Gospels is expected to understand the miracles of Jesus in a literal sense. And talking of sense, while I agree that Davidson's interpretation makes more sense, if the story built up around the historical Jesus is a myth, we should not expect complete sense. The myth is a grand metaphor, but if we do not accept the reality behind the metaphor, we miss the whole point of the myth.

So, if Jesus did all the things he is said to have done, naturally enough people talked. This man was supposed to be the Messiah, the one who had been so long awaited. He was the Son of God. Very probably Jesus himself was not the originator of the story, although I suspect that in the end he did come to half-believe some of the things that were being said about him, and at times he did get carried away by all the dreams spinning round and round in his head. Some pertinent information is supplied by Matthew when he tells us this:

Now when Jesus came into the district of Caesarea Philippi, he asked his disciples, 'Who do men say that the Son of man is?' And they said, 'Some say John the Baptist, others say Elijah, and others Jeremiah or one of the prophets.' He said to them, 'But who do you say that I am?' Simon Peter replied, 'You are the Christ, the Son of the living God.' And Jesus answered him, 'Blessed are you, Simon Bar-Jona! For flesh and blood has not revealed this to you, but my Father who is in heaven.'

Matthew 16: 13–17

It would appear, then, that Peter knew more than the others about those dreams in his Master's head, and Jesus was highly pleased with him. For to my mind, Jesus was not testing his disciples; he was questioning the growing suspicions he had in his more lucid moments about his own identity. How much of what he was hearing about himself could be true? He must have known that there could be no incontrovertible answer. But truth or lies, sense or non-sense, through it all there emerges the figure of a very great personality whose fame has endured for over two thousand years.

Certainly the myth has done a great deal for him. It has blown his importance out of all proportion. And people's infatuation with their God-man has brought with it calamities as well as benefits. But then, there are so many stupid people in the world, if it were not Jesus, it would be someone else. Jesus can not be expected to take the blame.

But in the end he did have to take the blame for the 'crimes' he was alleged to have committed. His accusers said that he had claimed to be the King of the Jews. Herod the King, and the Romans who had installed him, were not standing for that, and the Jews in high places spurred them on. The Roman procurator, Pontius Pilate, had nothing for it but to pronounce the death sentence, even though he himself could see no fault in the man brought before him. Jesus was led away to Golgotha and crucified.

Certainly that is no myth. It has been attested by Josephus, and those other historians I have already mentioned. A man called Jesus was actually crucified in the time of the Emperor Tiberius.

That is the firm faith of all believers. But there have always been unbelievers.

The Church Father Irenaeus, who was bishop of Hieropolis in Asia Minor around 120 CE, and who might have been expected to believe every word of the Gospels, did not hold with this story. Although we should remember that the four Gospels as we have them had not yet been put together by the selection of material from all the various manuscripts in circulation at the time. The first complete manuscripts of the Gospels date no further back than the fourth century AD, as the earlier manuscripts on papyrus have perished with time, and most of the later ones on vellum have been burnt by the enemies of Christianity. And so what we do have could be very far from the truth as given in the originals. There are arguments against this contention, but it is certain that however much of the text we are left with may be true, we can never be sure that it is. Irenaeus would not have had any reason to question the authority of the Gospels that were known to him, yet he maintained that Jesus lived to be an old man who died in his bed, and he gives the apostle John as warrant for his claim. And Papias, also a bishop, held the same belief as Irenaeus.

If we take a good hard look at the Gospel story we may come to the same opinion, for these are the facts:

when Jesus was taken off for burial in the tomb of Joseph of Arimathea, he was the only one of the three crucified whose legs were not broken because, it was affirmed, he was already dead; though this was a matter of some surprise to Pilate, for death by crucifixion was normally a long-drawn-out business, and although the three had to be taken down before the Sabbath, which was the day following, it was not expected that any of them would yet be dead. And the likely conclusion is that the other two, unfed and unable to move, died in due course, while Jesus, still under the influence of the benumbing potion he had been given to relieve his suffering, was taken off in a heavy coma which had all the appearance of death, and was buried in a tomb in which its owner did not intend to let him remain. Perhaps the guards allowed themselves to be persuaded, by some financial inducement, to look the other way; somehow his disciples contrived to make off with Jesus to a secret hide-out, maybe the Essene settlement at Qumran, where he ultimately recovered, and from which he was able to carry on with his work, if in a different fashion, for many years. And if this is what really did happen, then it would account for his several appearances to his disciples after his 'death'.

Both Irenaeus and Papias might have come by some foundation for their belief from the Gospel of Thomas, unearthed at Nag Hammâdi in Egypt in 1945. Thomas, one of Jesus' twelve apostles, has nothing whatever to say about the crucifixion of his Master, nor about his resurrection; and that is odd, to say the least.

The oddities abound, but the story as we have it in the Gospels is all we have to go on, and all there is to argue about. Well, not all, but it is the only complete story, and the only compelling one. Whether or not it is true, I base my argument on the supposition (and it can be no more than that) that, in the main, it is. And I ask your pardon for all the necessary repetition that follows.

This, then, is the gist of the story:

Jesus – the Jesus of the Gospels – was born of a virgin in Bethlehem of Judaea in the reign of Herod, tetrarch of Galilee. A devout man called Simeon had had revealed to him by the Holy Spirit that he would not see death before he had seen the Lord's Christ, and in the temple at Jerusalem, where he first set eyes on the baby Jesus, he ecstatically hailed him as 'a light for revelation to the Gentiles, and the glory of all Israel'. This baby was smuggled into Egypt in order to escape the hounding of Herod who wanted him dead, for he was troubled by all the talk of a coming King of the Jews. After Herod's death Jesus was brought back to his own country where he lived in Nazareth in Galilee with his mother Mary and Joseph, her husband, the local carpenter.

When Jesus was twelve years old he went with his parents to Jerusalem for the feast of the Passover, and he had many questions to put to the teachers in the temple there, and they were astounded to find such great wisdom in so young a boy. When the feast was over his parents set out with all the other pilgrims on the homeward journey, and they supposed that Jesus was among the crowd. When they discovered that he was not, they went back to Jerusalem to find him, and when they found him, in the porch of the temple, questioning and arguing with the teachers, they rebuked him.

And his mother said to him, 'Son, why have you done this to us? Your father and I have looked everywhere for you and we were worried about you.' And he said to them, 'Why were you looking for me? Did you not know that I must be about my Father's business?'

Luke 2: 48–49

There is nothing more told about Jesus until he was a grown man, except for some whimsical childhood stories in the Apocryphal Gospels.

At the age of thirty he was baptized in the River Jordan by his cousin, John the Baptist, after which he set out on his ministry. During his travels about the country he gathered all sorts of people around him, and among those closest to him were the beloved disciple and Mary Magdalene, who was a prostitute. He attracted large crowds and performed many miracles. Some people liked him and some didn't. From the beginning the temple authorities were against him. They didn't like the way he spoke to them, and they didn't hold with the precepts he taught; they were suspicious of all the wonders he was said to have performed; and they didn't like the stories that were going about concerning him: that he was the Messiah, the Son of God, and the King of the Jews. They turned this last claim into the chief reason for his arrest by the Roman authorities, who had installed Herod as King of the Jews, and in the end Jesus was apprehended and given some sort of trial, and finally was led away to Golgotha (Calvary) and crucified. After his death he was buried in a tomb belonging to Joseph of Arimathea, but when certain of his disciples visited the tomb, they found that the body was gone. Jesus had risen from the dead, as he had always said he would. The Word made flesh, the very God incarnate, could not be subject to the indignity of death. Jesus lives on for ever.

That is the end of the story. But it is just the beginning of a new one. My story.

Let us return to Golgotha where Jesus is dying on the cross. For it is just at that point, at the very end, that we are able to uncover the secret which has been puzzling us from the beginning: who was the beloved disciple?

The only one of the evangelists to throw any light on the subject is John, and he is the one reckoned by many to be that disciple.

According to his own account, among those standing round the cross at Jesus' crucifixion were his mother, his mother's sister, Mary the wife of Clopas, Mary Magdalene, and the beloved disciple. Mary of Nazareth, his mother, who had never been close to him in life, would naturally be there at his death, and since she had given him no cause to cast her off, he felt it was no less than his duty as a son to make some provision for her. Joseph, her husband, who was much older than she was, was almost certainly dead, and those 'brothers' the Gospels speak of, if they were in fact brothers of his, were probably half-brothers, Joseph's sons by his first wife. So Jesus decided then and there to put his mother into the care of the one person he knew he could count on, the 'beloved disciple'. Surely a man. He could hardly have given her over to a woman.

As the Gospel puts it:

When Jesus saw his mother, and the disciple whom he loved standing near, he said to his mother, 'Woman, this is your son!' Then he said to the disciple, 'This is your mother!' And from then on the disciple took her to *his* home. [The italics are mine.]

John 19: 26–27

The identity of the 'disciple whom Jesus loved' is still not revealed, but whether he is John or any other, or whether he is a mythical figure or not, surely there is conclusive evidence that he can't be Mary Magdalene.

And when Jesus said his final farewell to his beloved, Mary must have realized how blind she had been. But I don't believe that Jesus would have forgotten her. He probably had something to say to her too by way of condolence and belated apology, though there is nothing recorded. He must have known that the inevitable conclusion of his Agony would be the end of the agony for her. If that was any consolation to him.

And that, as his accusers thought, was the end of Jesus. They could never have foreseen what was to come. If they had had any conception of the momentous nature of the train of events they were setting in motion, they would most likely have let him be. The God-man rose from the dead, to prove his claim that he was God's Son. God is immortal; He cannot die; and had not Jesus said 'I and the Father are one'? The Son, the Logos had returned to the bosom of His Father.

It was one of the three who were missing him most who made the discovery.

Now on the first day of the week Mary Magdalene came to the tomb early, while it was still dark, and saw that the stone had been taken away from the tomb. So she ran, and went to Simon Peter and the other disciple, the one whom Jesus loved, and said to them, 'They have taken the Lord out

72

of the tomb, and we do not know where they have laid him.' Peter then came out with the other disciple, and they went toward the tomb. They both ran, but the other disciple outran Peter and reached the tomb first; and stooping to look in, he saw the linen cloths lying there, but he did not go in. Then Simon Peter came, following him, and went into the tomb; he saw the linen cloths lying, and the napkin, which had been on his head, not lying with the linen cloths but rolled up in a place by itself. Then the other disciple, who reached the tomb first, also went in and he saw and believed.

John 20: 1–8

He believed that Jesus was risen, but what else he believed, or knew about his Master is open to question. People have always had divergent opinions.

And not just about Jesus' personal life. Also about the meaning of his message. Gnostics have always sought to demonstrate that Jesus was one of them, and they have interpreted his sayings very plausibly to that effect. Even so, as I have already stated, I cannot agree with them.

Jesus was a well-educated man, quite obviously, and it is unlikely that he would not have been acquainted with at least some of the writings of the great mystics such as Orpheus, Pythagoras, Plato, Socrates, Valentinus, Colarbasus, Marcus, Elchasai, Heraclitus, Clement of Alexandria, Jesus Ben Sirach. He could hardly have been unfamiliar with the works and ideas of Philo Jedaeus, who was such a renowned Hellenistic philosopher of his own time. If indeed he had been a member of the Essene fraternity, he most certainly would not. And he would have known that Philo did not

73

believe that the Logos, or Word, could become incarnate in any one man. It is the essence of the divine in every man. What Jesus would have thought of that we cannot know, but he would have been very greatly interested in what all these men had to say; but it was not what *he* wanted to say. His message was not for the few; it was for all who were prepared to listen to him. It is true that there is much to be found in his sayings that is of a profoundly mystical nature, but it does not require a whole lot of elucidation for the intelligent listener, or reader, to grasp his meaning; although in some cases his meaning has been 'improved upon' by those who thought they knew better. To these I can just hear Jesus speaking these words which I am putting into his mouth:

Alas for you, Gnostics, you who see yourselves as men of the higher wisdom. You are not liars, neither are you hypocrites. You do not seek to deceive, but you are deceived. For your lies are by their very nature a fabrication hiding in its own complexity; truth is simple and one. I send my words out into the bright sunlight; yours are hid under a dark cloud. When darkness falls, do not men retire to their rest and sleep? And except in the illusion of a dream they see nothing more until the darkness is gone. Then, when the sun shines in the heavens, then they awake and their eyes see all the things that were hidden from them before. If your heavenly Father had not sent the sun to give you light, you would dwell in darkness for ever. Of all His great gifts to you, there is no greater.

When a Gnostic sets about revealing what the eye

cannot see or the mind contemplate, his tongue cannot speak plainly but must always veil his meaning under a cloud. He knows that if he is to say what he means, it will never mean what he says unless he speaks in allegory and metaphor. But even a Gnostic can only see what he is able to see and understand. What he can never understand, or imagine, he will never see. And what he thinks he sees can be no more than a mystic dream. But whatever Jesus may have said to those closest to him, which might well have been somewhat different from what he said to the crowd, he would still have wanted it to be understood in its intrinsic nature, and in general he wished to be seen as an ordinary man speaking to ordinary men in an ordinary language. His intention was always to make himself clear.

If he had gone in for so-called 'secret teachings', he would have had to divide his practice between preaching to the common people, by way of parable and straight talking, and mystical discourses reserved for initiates, among whom I do not see the fishermen from the Lake of Galilee who were his first disciples. Moreover, his double message would have given his listeners considerable disquiet. What was he actually saying? And if what they thought he was saying was good enough for the majority, why did he feel he should treat the others differently? As is well known, large crowds hung about to hear him preach. I hardly think that would have been the case if he had had very much to say about things mystical. They listened to him because they were interested in what he had to say. If he had gone on and on about 'principalities', 'powers', the 'heavenly hierarchy', the 'Aeon of Aeons', and such like, they would soon have given him up as a bad job. As they would have done if they had suspected that he was keeping all that for the select few. He could not have it both ways. And I don't believe he ever wanted to.

Jesus was indeed able to see the mystical reality behind the physical world, but he was a practical man who never denied the reality of everyday life. On more than one occasion, when his challengers do their utmost to make things awkward for him, he is not the mystical figure of a Gnostic's imagining; he is the real man who is always one-up on his challengers; the clever man, the very clever man – much too clever for the myth – who is determined not to be caught out.

But there were always those equally determined to catch him out. There was so much talk of a coming Messiah, and so many claiming to be that one, Jesus was forever being hard-pressed to reveal his true identity. Was he this Messiah or was he a clever charlatan?

When the chief priests and elders demanded of him,

'By what authority are you doing these things, and who gave you this authority?'

he was one jump ahead of them. He said to them,

'I also will ask you a question, and if you can tell me the answer, then I also will tell you by what authority I do these things. The baptism of John, did it come from heaven or from men?'

Matthew 21: 24–25

And Matthew goes on:

They argued with one another, 'If we say "From heaven", he will say to us, "Why then did you not

76

believe him?" But if we say, "From men", we are afraid of the people; for they maintain that John was a prophet.' So they answered Jesus, 'We do not know.' And he said to them, 'Neither will I tell you by what authority I do these things.'

Matthew 21: 25–27

Jesus was not to be caught out.

Matthew gives another equally good story in chapter 22:

Then the Pharisees went off and put their heads together to see if they could find a way to make him say something he regretted. And they sent their disciples to him, together with the Herodians, to say, 'Master, we know that you are an honest man and teach the way of God in an honest way, and that you are not afraid of anyone, because a man's rank means nothing to you. Tell us your opinion, then. Is it lawful to pay taxes to Caesar or not?' But Jesus could see through them; he replied 'You hypocrites! Why do you set this trap for me? Let me see the money you pay the tax with.' They handed him a denarius, and he said, 'Whose head is this? Whose name?' 'Caesar's' they replied. He then said to them, 'Well, then, give to Caesar what belongs to Caesar – and to God what belongs to God.' They were not expecting this reply; they turned from him and went on their way.

Matthew 22: 15–22

They knew they had met more than their match. But they never gave up. This from John:

77

The scribes and the Pharisees brought a woman who had been caught in adultery, and placing her in the midst they said to him, 'Teacher, this woman has been caught in the act of adultery. Now in the law Moses commanded us to stone such. What do you say about her?' This they said to test him, that they might have some charge to bring against him. Jesus bent down and wrote with his finger on the ground. And as they continued to ask him, he stood up and said to them, 'Let him who is without sin among you be the first to throw a stone at her.' And once more he bent down and wrote with his finger on the ground.

John 8: 3–8

He obviously had to think hard about that one, but as usual he proved equal to the task; and

When they heard it, they went away, one by one, beginning with the eldest.

That old man was saying all that needed to be said. But I would like to say something too. On this occasion, as on so many others, Jesus does not show himself as the 'distant, inhuman person who was God-in-disguise,' as Kuhn saw him. Seen from where I stand, Jesus is not speaking to those scribes and Pharisees as a perfect God-man to common sinners; he is the normal man who knows what it is to sin, as they do, even if they are better at it! He is not asking to be made a part of any myth.

Always displaying great caution, after he has performed some miracle he requires the benefactors to tell no one. Which, I have to say, does seem to me rather silly.

78

Naturally people would talk, and anyone who had known a man crippled and unable to walk, and had then seen him walking about like anyone else, would want an explanation. As he would if he saw a man who had died alive again. And, as well, the participants in such a myth as that one about the adulteress would not be doing anything to denigrate their hero, and the hero of the other myths would not be at any time less wise than Solomon.

And I can think of another instance where Jesus, for all his caution, and his cleverness, doesn't quite make it:

> As he passed by, he saw a man who had been blind from his birth. And his disciples asked him, 'Rabbi, who sinned, this man or his parents, that he was born blind?' Jesus answered, 'It was not that this man sinned, or his parents, but that the works of God might be revealed in him. We must work the works of him who sent me, while it is day; night comes, when no one can work. As long as I am in the world, I am the light of the world.'
>
> John 9: 1–5

The disciples who asked Jesus that question may not have been testing him; just seeking some sort of explanation for this one instance of the many unexplained conundrums this life presents us with. But the question would have been appropriate coming from one of the Pharisees. Jesus' reply does, as always, reveal his higher wisdom, but at the risk of being labelled an imbecile, I must say that it does not make all that much sense to me. I wonder what his questioners made of it. And still more I wonder what the blind man made of it.

Yet, in spite of his usual caution, at times Jesus adopts a very different attitude. In the words of J R Porter in his book *Jesus Christ – The Jesus of History, the Christ of Faith*:

> Jesus repeatedly says that God is unknown and unknowable to human beings (John 5: 37, 6: 46) but is revealed in His Son, and that this is the whole purpose of his ministry.

Plainly Jesus is asserting that he himself is that Son. And he has no hesitation in saying so.

And Matthew's Gospel gives us this: after he has told a young hopeful that however good a life he has lived, if he wants to be perfect and so deserving of eternal life, he must sell everything he possesses and give the money to the poor, and go and follow him, then, when that young man, who 'had great possessions', went away despairing, Jesus said to his disciples,

> 'Truly, I tell you, it will be hard for a rich man to enter the kingdom of heaven. Again I tell you, it is easier for a camel to go through the eye of a needle than for a rich man to enter the kingdom of God.'

> Matthew 19: 23–24

So, then, naturally, they all wondered what chance any of them had. And Peter protested:

> 'We have left everything and followed you. What then shall be our lot?'

> Matthew 19: 27

And here is Jesus' reply:

> 'Truly I tell you, that you who have followed me,
> in the regeneration when the Son of man shall sit
> in the throne of his glory, you also shall sit upon
> twelve thrones, judging the twelve tribes of Israel.
> And every one who has left behind their houses,
> or their brothers, or sisters, or father, or mother,
> or wife, or children, or lands, for my name's sake,
> shall receive a hundredfold, and shall inherit
> everlasting life.'
>
> Matthew 19: 27–29

There, quite apart from his appalling lack of sympathy
for those brothers and sisters, fathers and mothers, wives
and children, Jesus again shows no reluctance at all to
speak out. He has thrown all caution to the winds. But
it does seem to me that in this instance he has gone
too far in the other direction. He has come to believe
what he wants to believe, and even some of his followers
have believed it too. And always will.

For the myth that has been built around the man
Jesus is for every time and everywhere, and it is one
that we men, and women, cannot do without.

As Tom Harpur, in *The Pagan Christ*, puts it, so
much better than I ever could:

> The central figure represents both the Christos
> (Divine Principle as he/it incarnates and dies only
> to rise again in self-offering on behalf of all human-
> kind), *and also the soul of every individual in its*
> *journey to eternal life.*

And then:

81

The story of Jesus is the story of each of us in allegorical form. As spirit-gifted animals, we are crucified on the cross of matter; we are bearers of the Christ within and will one day be resurrected to a glorious destiny with God.

But if we cannot do without the myth, can we do without the man? Jesus' story is told in the Gospels as a straightforward story, and we can believe it or not believe it as we please. And indeed we should be very foolish to believe the whole of it. But belief in the reality of Jesus himself has persisted for centuries, and if only for that reason we have a clear warrant to take an interest in the man, as in any other famous person. Only this famous person is something more. As Harpur puts it:

The Gospels are really dramas about the Christos, with Jesus in the starring role as a dramatic personality. Jesus is the symbolic personification of the Christos.

Well, although Harpur seems to be implying that Jesus is no more than a symbol, if we could take him to mean that the *real man* Jesus should be *understood* as that symbol, then I would go along with him. Mary's interest in Jesus had its other side. Perhaps ours should too.

There, I have had my say. I can't prove that any of it is true, neither can anyone else prove that it isn't. As Gorgias the Greek philosopher and sophist said:

What is right but what we prove to be right? And what is truth but what we believe to be truth?

82

We are stuck with that. But as a rule people will believe what they see with their own eyes. I haven't seen Jesus, but I have listened to him, and it has *seemed* to me that I was looking deep into his eyes, and what I saw there was the man as I have portrayed him. I can't say fairer than that. And if I have shown him up to be less than perfect, that is as it must be, for no man is perfect, and Jesus was a man. But for all his imperfections, he was a very good man, and a very great one, and when I look into his eyes he looks back into mine and he smiles. A man such as he is has no stomach for a lie; he is no pretender; if he knows he is right, he will stand up for himself against anyone at all, but if you can show him where he is wrong, he will thank you for it. As we are given to understand, God is Love. But the way I would have it, God is Truth. And Jesus, as His Son (*as* standing for *in the role of*), is an integral part of that Truth.

Epilogue

Whatever I may appear to *think* about Jesus, the following two poems should leave you in no doubt as to my true feelings towards him. The first, written under my maiden name of Mary Christina St John, can be found in the sacred section of my *Collected Poems* published by the Book Guild in 2007; the second, the reaction brought on by my assessment of the character of Jesus necessary for the writing of this book, has come too late for inclusion in the collection, but is not, I think, out of place here.

LOVE-SONG

I had a True-Love long, long ago
that to my bitter chagrin I forsook
for lover-boys who valued me far less;
for in my self-delusion I mistook
the moment's ravishment for happiness
that was humiliation, pain and sorrow.

But my True-Love was patient and bore with me,
though I made no attempt to hide my shame;
He showed not the slightest trace of jealousy,
nor even once sought to apportion blame.
Of course I knew well who should bear the blame,
but went on cheating on Him just the same.

Until the time came, as it always must,
my crazy craving burnt out and turned to dust.
Tail between my legs, I crawled back then,
with the nerve to hope He'd take me back again.
But a mere hope it was, and nothing more,
that sent me timidly knocking at His door.

'I know I have no business here,' I said.
'I have betrayed you and defiled your bed.
If you want no more of me, I'll understand.'
But 'No,' He said, and gently took my hand,
'remember our compact when we two were wed.
The pain you suffer now is my pain too.
How can you think I could ever stop loving you?'

A CONFESSION

Ah, God, I love your Son, and well I know
that He loves me. I cannot ask for more.
There is no more in heaven or here below,
and I am at peace now as never I was before
when, young, with blinkered eyes I could not see
the pre-eminence of the One that most loved me.

This love is something else. Indeed I never
thought that it would come to this: that I
would fall in love again, that I could ever
so debase myself to live a lie
like all those silly old women who cannot admit
love's dream is over, and there's an end of it.

But this is no dream; this is more real than real;
it will not fade with the coming of the light.
The light is with me now. The joy I feel,
like the bright sun, combats the shades of night.
My night of age has turned to glorious day.
The True-Love that I hold is here to stay.
The new life that is mine will never pass away.

If you think I should make up my mind which one I am asking you to believe in – the real man Jesus or the mythical Incarnate Son – my answer is: you must please yourself; but as far as I am concerned they are one and the same.

Bibliography

Baigent, Michael, Leigh, Richard, and Lincoln, Henry, *The Holy Blood and the Holy Grail* (Century Publishing, 2005)

Brown, Dan, *The Da Vinci Code* (Doubleday, 2003)

Davidson, John, *The Gospel of Jesus* (Element Books, 1995)

Doherty, Earl, *The Jesus Puzzle* (Canadian Humanist Publications, 1999)

Drews, Arthur, *The Christ Myth* (1910)

Freke, Timothy and Gandy, Peter, *The Laughing Jesus* (Harmony Books, 2005)

Frye, Northrop, *The Double Vision, Language and Meaning in Religion* (University of Toronto Press, 1991)

Harpur, Tom, *The Pagan Christ* (Thomas Allen Publishers, 2004)

Josephus, Flavius, Ed Maier, Paul, *The New Complete Works of Josephus* (Kregel Publications, 1999)

Kuhn, Alvin Boyd, *Who is this King of Glory?* (Academy Press, 1944)

Massey, Gerald, 'Luniolatry, Ancient and Modern' in *Lectures* (1887)

   The Historical Jesus and the Mythical Christ (Star Publishing, 1886)

   The Natural Genesis (Williams and Norgate, 1883)

Picknett, Lynn and Prince, Clive, *The Templar Revelation* (Bantam Press, 1997)

Porter, J.R., *Jesus Christ; The Jesus of History, The Christ of Faith* (Duncan Baird, 1999)

Renan, Ernest, *The Life of Jesus* (1863)

Strauss, David Friedrich, *Life of Jesus* (first published 1902, latest edition, Kessinger Publishing, 2008)

Thiering, Barbara, *Jesus the Man; New Interpretation from the Dead Sea Scrolls* (Corgi Books, 1993)

Wilson, Ian, *Jesus – The Evidence* (Weidenfeld and Nicolson, 1996)

Index

Aitken, Johan L. 6
Alexandria, Clement of 73
Alexandria, the library 8
Arimathea, Joseph of 70
Arjus 4
Arjuna 12
Augustine, St 18
Augustus Caesar 5, 24

Baigent, Michael 50
Bethlehem 24
Bhagavad-Gita 12
blind man 79
Boussard, Colonel 8
Brown, Dan 49, 50
Buddha 34

Campbell, Joseph 43
Catacombs 11
Centurion 47
Chalcedon 3
Champollion 8
Christos 9, 81, 82
Colarbasus 73
Constantine, Emperor 16

David, King 24, 28
Davidson, John 22, 31, 36, 40, 64
Dionysus 17
Disciple whom Jesus loved 42,
    51, 56, 59, 60, 71, 72
Docetes 3

Doherty, Earl 7
Drews, Arthur 2

Eckhard, Meister 2
Elchasai 73
Ephraim 28
Essenes 28, 60

Fig tree 28
Freke, Timothy 2, 25, 43
Freud, Sigmund 20
Frye, Northrop 6

Gandy, Peter 2, 25, 43
Gnostics 73, 74, 75
Gorgias 82

Harpur, Tom 5, 9, 11, 15, 16,
    19, 81, 82
Heraclitus 73
Herod Antipas 28
Herod the Great 16, 66, 70
Heroditus 14
Higgins, Godfrey 4, 20
homosexuality 56
Horus 10, 11, 12, 13, 14

Irenaeus 56, 67
Isis 11, 15
Iusu 13, 14

Jesus Ben Sirach 73

Jesus Seminar 35
Joanna, wife of Chuza 53
John, the apostle 60, 67, 71
John the Baptist 28, 50, 61
Joseph, father of Jesus 24, 60, 69, 71
Joseph of Arimathea 68, 70
Josephus 30

Krishna 12
Kuhn, Alvin Boyd 5, 9, 11, 17, 18, 19, 78

Lazarus 28, 58
Leigh, Richard 50
Lincoln, Henry 50
Logos 9, 17, 20, 36, 40, 74
Luxor, the temple 10, 11, 17

Magi 11
Manasseh 8, 28
Mani 12
Marcus 73
Mark, Secret Gospel 57, 58
Martyr, Justin 14
Mary Magdalene 35, 49, 50, 71, 72
Mary, Martha's sister 28
Mary, mother of Jesus 41
Mary, wife of Clopas 71
Massey, Gerald 4, 10, 17, 23
Mithras 11
Monophysites 3
Muhammad 34
Mystery religions 7, 40

Nag Hammâdi codices 37
Nazarenes 60
Nicene Creed 4, 51
Nudity 57

Orpheus 73
Orphism 40

Osiris 10

Papias 67
Paul, St 20, 35, 54
Peter, Simon 35, 51, 66, 73
Philip 49
Philo 6, 73
Picknett, Lynn 52
plagiarism 15, 20
Plato 40, 73
Pliny the Elder 33
Pliny the Younger 33
Pontius Pilate 67
Porter J.R. 80
Prince, Clive 52
Prometheus 14
Pythagoras 40, 73

Qumran 28

Ra 17
Renan, Ernest 2
Retractiones 18
Rosetta Stone 8

Salivahana 12
Schweizer, Albert 20
Simeon 69
Smith, Dr Morton 57
Socrates 73
Strauss, David Friedrich 35
Suetonius 32
Susanna 53
Syrophoenician woman 46, 47

Tacitus 32, 33
Talmud 41
Temple, cleansing 34, 45
Tertullian, Quintus 15
Thiering, Barbara 27
Thomas, apostle 37, 68
Thomas, Gospel 26, 37, 57, 68
Tiberius 23, 24, 30

Trajan, Emperor 33

Valentinus 73

Wilson, Ian 57

Word 36, 40, 41

Zarathustra 11
Zend-Avesta 11
Zoroaster 11